A TIME TO LAUGH

My Life over Fifty

LISA J. RADCLIFF

ILLUSTRATIONS BY
KARISSA MURMYLO

ISBN 979-8-88685-890-7 (paperback)
ISBN 979-8-88685-891-4 (digital)

Copyright © 2023 by Lisa J. Radcliff

All rights reserved. No part of this publication may be reproduced, distributed, or transmitted in any form or by any means, including photocopying, recording, or other electronic or mechanical methods without the prior written permission of the publisher. For permission requests, solicit the publisher via the address below.

Christian Faith Publishing
832 Park Avenue
Meadville, PA 16335
www.christianfaithpublishing.com

Printed in the United States of America

Endorsements for A Time to Laugh

I am not sure if I love this devotional so much because I am a fella-quinquagenarian or because it's just plain good! *A Time to Laugh:My Life Over Fifty* captures the highs and lows through the different seasons of your life from raising kids and grand-parenting to everything in-between. Lisa encourages you each day through ordinary and extraordinary moments. One minute you'll be laughing and the next crying as she shares tidbits of her own life and the lessons she learned along the way. You'll be inspired in your walk with God and with others—reflecting the insights you read each day!

Jessie Seneca
Author, Speaker
Founder of More of Him Ministries

"A cheerful heart is good medicine," Proverbs 17:22 NIV says. In *A Time to Laugh: My Life Over Fifty* Lisa Radcliff provides a healthy dose of humor and truth for women in their fifties and beyond. Give a copy to a friend—or yourself. It's sure to be appreciated. — Marlene Bagnull, Write His Answer Ministries

Marlene Bagnull
Author | Speaker | Editor | Publisher, Ampelos Press
Director, Write His Answer Ministries

I LOVE this book and this author! If you want to feel younger, smarter, more beautiful, and more loved--while laughing your head off, grab a daily dose from this hilarious "Quinquagenarian!" Made-up words, ridiculous stories that lead to deep spiritual insight and hope, that's what you'll find in these pages. Highly recommended!

Marnie Swedbcrg, Mentor to Millions, www.Marnie.com

This book is dedicated to Emma, Taylor, Sam, Morgan, Everlee, Noel, Isaiah, Harper, and Daniel—my precious grands who make me laugh every day. I have been blessed beyond measure!

Contents

Introduction

I am a quinquagenarian. A what? Don't worry, it's nothing contagious. It's just a big fun word for someone in their fifties. I thought I'd share some of the stories of my fifties so other quinquagenarians can know they are not alone in wondering what happened to their minds and bodies. Maybe laughing at my stories will allow you to laugh at your own.

I almost can't believe I have been alive for over fifty years, although my body tells a different story. That's a lot of living—a lot of smiles, tears, blessings, belly laughs, heartaches, and lessons learned. It also means I have arrived in a season of life when I have more years to look back on than to look forward to. I don't consider that a sad statement. Since I can see God's faithfulness in the past, it's easy to believe he will be faithful in the future. My fifties brought a mixture of positive and negative circumstances but also a decade of fun and laughter.

While having the typical aches and pains that come after age fifty, of which I experience liberally, some of the stories in this book were written as I was going through a health crisis. Even through that, God gave me times of rejoicing and laughter. Some of the laughter came from the people he has put in my life: friends, family, grandchildren, and others. I'm at that magical age where I can enjoy my adult children and spoil my grandchildren. Of special interest (to me, at least) are the quotes from my grandchildren. The littles in my life are a constant source of joy, laughter, love, and blog fodder.

This season has given me more time to spend with friends, which is where the serious laughter takes place. With their permission, some of our crazy adventures are also included in this book, although my girlfriends may deny any connection to me. I am so blessed to be surrounded with other quinquagenarians (and some older—but don't tell them I said that) who share my sense of humor and love of laughter. My life would be much less without them as would my abdominal muscles (from lack of belly laughs). I also included stories from my childhood, raising my boys, and lessons I have learned in fifty-plus years.

Noticeably absent from a book about life as a quinquagenarian are stories related to menopause. There is a good reason for that: I haven't experienced it yet. That in itself is pretty hilarious since I'm closing in on sixty years old. Perhaps those fun moments will be in a future book on being a woman in her sixties. Let's hope so.

Every story is true and barely embellished. Most of the time, my experiences taught me a spiritual lesson or reminded me of a biblical principle or Scripture passage, which I hope will encourage or challenge you. Some stories are a little more serious, and some of them are just fun stories. Go ahead and laugh, cry, and celebrate life.

Being a quinquagenarian is fantastic. If you are in those magical years of fifty to sixty, I hope you smile as you relate to the stories from my life. I also hope they lighten the burdens you may be experiencing. And if you're not there yet, consider this book preparation for some of the best years of your life.

AGING

Emma: This game is for four-year-olds and…how old are you, Mom-mom?
Me: Fifty-three.
Emma: …and fifty-three-year-olds.
Me: I'll be fifty-four next month.
Emma: Mom-mom, why are you counting?

A Tent Full of Trouble

I remember the little orange pup tent we had as kids, barely big enough for two of us to crawl in and sleep. During one camping trip, a thunderstorm rolled in. My worried dad kept coming from the camper to check on my sister and me, keeping us from getting to sleep. I finally said to my sister, "Don't answer him next time he comes out. He'll think we've fallen asleep and leave us alone." It worked. His overly protective visits stopped.

A little while later, my sister said, "I hope he wasn't trying to tell us something important like, 'your tent is on fire.'" We giggled ourselves to sleep.

Recently, I read in 2 Corinthians 5 that our bodies are tents and that they groan. That explains a lot. There's plenty of groaning going on with my body, and now I know why. *It's a tent*. The Coleman-lantern light bulb in my brain popped on. And as a fifty-plus-year-old with a cornucopia of orthopedic issues, *I hate* tent camping.

My tent has seen better days. It's no longer comfortable, even though it has more padding than it used to. For some reason, I think I can still sit for an extended period of time with one leg folded underneath me without any backlash. Standing up, my foot is not just asleep; it's in a coma. I go hobbling around the room with a familiar mantra, "Ow, ow, ow." My tent also has sprung some leaks. Coughing, laughing, sneezing—they've all become conduits to leaks.

Its shape has definitely changed—bulges, rolls, and wrinkles everywhere. It is not one of those tents that you pull open, and they pop right into place, all sleek and springy, without a single wrinkle.

I admit, when I was a kid, it was fun to sleep outside in our pup tent. It was an adventure. As I got older, the allure faded. I slept in a tent in our backyard one time when my boys were young. I hated it. Our hard Pennsylvania clay is not meant for sleeping on. I was sure the rock poking me all night was alive, following me, as I rolled to and fro, trying to find a soft spot. Finally, around 4:00 a.m., I thought, *This is ridiculous. My comfortable bed is two hundred feet away. What am I doing out here?* I retreated to my nice, soft Serta with no rocks and no regrets.

A new trend has gained popularity, probably because of people like me who raise an eyebrow at going camping. It's called glamping. It stands for "glamorous camping." You still sleep in a tent, but it is considered luxurious. They have real, queen-size beds with 1,500-thread-count Egyptian cotton sheets. They come with electricity and even chandeliers. I don't know. If it comes with a private bathroom featuring hot water, a soaker tub, and some cinnamon-scented candles, maybe I would consider it.

My idea of glamping would include the word Disney somewhere in the description. If Disney did glamping, it would probably be okay. Have you noticed there are no bugs on Disney properties? Somebody bibbidi-bobbidi-booed them off the premises. It's not glamping if it's not critter-free.

Second Corinthians 5:1 gives us great news concerning our tents, "for we know that if the earthly house, which is our tent, is torn down, we have a building from God, a house not made with hands, eternal in the heavens." Yes, right now my tent is groaning. It is also snapping, crackling, and popping, so it is with eager anticipation I set my gaze on the day it will be torn down. I don't know when that will be. I haven't seen an expiration date, but I'm pretty sure the warranty has run out. My new tent will be a glorified body. There will be no comparison with this earthly tent or my pup tent. I'll be glamping with Jesus.

It's Better to Have and Not Need...a Memory

I have started a new routine. I take all of my medications and supplements out of the cabinet and line them up on my kitchen counter. Then as I take each one, I set it aside or back in the cabinet. I find that if I don't do that, I forget which ones I took and which ones I have yet to take. And so many of them look alike. Sometimes, if I wasn't sure, I figured it was better to take two than none, so down the hatch—probably not a good idea.

A good memory has never been one of my strong suits. In elementary school, twice a week, we had band practice before school. I'd get up extra early and get to school for band practice. Walking in the door, I would realize I didn't have my clarinet with me. What did I think I was going early to school to do? There was only one thing—band practice. I spent a lot of time during band practice at the chalkboard, writing, "It is better to have and not need than to need and not have."

I am fascinated by the human brain. How does memory work? How does the brain forget a person's name but know the letter the name starts with? And if you haven't thought about it all day, how does it come up with the name at 3:00 a.m.? Was it searching through files the whole time? I worked for a lawyer whose office was in a converted house. He had files in every nook and cranny of that house. I actually filed things in the bathtub—not kidding. I think that's what my brain must look like.

I have had two MRIs of my brain. Both times, they said they didn't find anything. I'm not surprised. Then they tacked on, "There are two white spots. We don't know what they are, but they seem stable." I know what they are. That's where I keep all the information that would make my life easier, but I can't remember it.

As I've gotten older, my memory has gotten even worse. This actually happened as we were getting ready to go to leave the house.

My husband said, "Have you seen my sunglasses?"

I said, "They were on the dresser the last time I saw them."

He looked at me and said, "Really, 'cause they are on the top of your head."

"They are?" I took them off and looked at them. They were his. "Then where are mine?"

"In your hand," and the giggles spilled out.

That's me, panicked because I don't remember where I put my cell phone while I'm talking on it. And of course, the quintessential "what did I come in this room for?" *Every* day. I am thankful that I have started using the calendar alarm on my phone so at least I'm not missing important appointments. Now if I could just find my phone.

> So I will always remind you of these things, even though you know them and are firmly established in the truth you now have. I think it is right to refresh your memory as long as I live in the tent of this body, because I know that I will soon put it aside, as our Lord Jesus Christ has made clear to me. (2 Peter 1:12–14 ESV)

Loft Dressing

I will rejoice greatly in the LORD, My soul will be
joyful in my God; For He has clothed me with
garments of salvation, He has wrapped me with a
robe of righteousness. (Isaiah 61:10 ESV)

We have a little cabin in the backwoods of Maine. It's a special place
filled with memories and spiders, both live large. It's a place that time
hasn't changed. I love that. There seems to be an unwritten rule that
we can't buy new things for the cabin. In fact, if things purchased for
use at the cabin aren't already ancient, rusty, or unable to be used for
their original purpose, they don't belong there.

The cabin was built in 1974. Every piece of furniture in it was
used before 1974. That would include the mattresses. The mattress
in the master bedroom made the six-hundred-mile journey from
Pennsylvania tied to the trunk of a 1964 baby blue Impala. With the
convertible top down, it fitted perfectly.

Over the years, in a less than valiant attempt to make the mattress more comfortable, layers of memory foam, egg crate foam, and
plain old foam were added on top. They don't help, which is why my
husband and I sleep in the loft on another old mattress, directly on
the plywood floor. While my body has added layers of its own, they
have about the same effect as the layers of foam. But at least the loft
mattress doesn't scoot off the bottom of the bed when I rolled over.

I always slept in the loft as a kid, so it is rather nostalgic. It's the
perfect place to hear the loons calling or the rain on the roof. But
now, in my midfifties, it is getting a little more difficult and just a tad
painful. The only way into and out of the loft is via a ladder. Going

up is not too bad. But coming down usually takes place in the morning (or sometimes a special trip in the middle of the night) when muscles and joints are not quite at their optimum range of motion. The creaking and popping of those first few precarious steps cause me to stop and wonder if it's the forty-year-old handmade wooden ladder or me.

When my husband and I visit the cabin alone, we sleep in the loft but use the bedroom as our dressing room. On this trip, every room, bed, and nook were occupied. So we had to have our suitcase in the loft with us. Sure, we could have taken our clothes to the outhouse to dress, but I got dressed in the loft growing up; surely, I could do it now.

My husband didn't even try. He's much smarter than me. He's also much taller. The loft is not a complete second floor. At 5'1", I am about 3" taller than the peak. But that's okay. As every female who has ever tried squeezing into freshly washed jeans knows, lying on the bed to put them on is the best way to go.

So there I was, lying on the worn-out mattress, pulling on jeans, squeezing and tucking, rolling and pulling, hoping not to break a hip. Then it happened. Lying on my back with everything tucked into place, the button slipped through the buttonhole like they were a size too big. *Wow, all the swimming and kayaking must be tightening my abs*, I thought. I laid there, like I was a teenager again, so proud of my flat stomach and the ease with which the two sides of my jeans came together. Then I sat up. Gravity and physics resumed their normal functions. The button digging into my now protruding belly reminded me that s'mores are best left as a sweet memory of younger days too. At least my bottom half was clothed.

Now for the top, sitting on my knees, I pulled off my pajama top and grabbed an appropriate undergarment. But how to get it on? In my current position of hunched over, the girls were headed south, checking out the muffin top that would make Betty Crocker proud. I couldn't stand up. Eyeing the bed, I thought how the muffin top disappeared when I was lying down. So back on the mattress I went. But now the girls were heading east and west, each off on their own frolic. I don't remember that happening when I was younger. And I don't think this is what Solomon had in mind when he said, "Your breasts are like two fawns that graze among the lilies." What would Jesus do? He would go after them one at a time. So I did and got them safely into the pen and closed the door. Finally, I pulled on a cooperative stretchy T-shirt and just laid there for a few minutes. I took a few deep breaths, stomach flat, the girls rising and falling (pointing north). I decided, tomorrow I would get dressed in the outhouse. What could possibly go wrong there?

Hidden Scars

"Where is your scar?" A friend was comparing our appendix surgery stories. She thought it strange that she had a scar on the left side of her abdomen if her appendix had been on the right side. My operating-room-nurse husband explained why surgeons go across rather than down to retrieve the little bugger.

That led to a discussion on scars. It was more of a monologue—me complaining about my abdomen full of scars, which I keep hidden from public view. I've had at least five abdominal surgeries. We decided that since my largest scar looks like railroad tracks running from my sternum to my belly button, I should get a little railroad-gate tattoo. And I could top it off with a belly button piercing with a little bell to signal the gate, maybe add a train—the engine on my belly and the caboose on my…caboose. My scars could be something that would make me smile and maybe even wear a bikini—*not*.

I spent this week at an intense conference on child sexual abuse. I realized through this conference that I have scars no one sees, even more than I knew were there. They would not even be visible in a bikini. They are very deep inside. On the outside, I look great. I smile and laugh and live life large. Like the scars on my Chattanooga Choo Choo belly, you will probably never see my deep emotional and spiritual scars. But I know they are there, constant reminders of the trauma I suffered.

There's no dressing up these scars, no tattoos for comic relief. But they have a purpose. They have made me not just who I am but a better version of who I am. Because of my scars, I am a more compassionate, empathetic person. I am able to walk with others who have similar scars and understand their pain. Most importantly, I learned that God sent his Son to comfort the brokenhearted. He was pleased to crush his own Son so that I could be healed through his wounds (Isaiah 53).

At Jesus's resurrection, his scars were still visible, even touchable, had Thomas taken him up on the offer. They had accomplished their purpose. While still evident, their time of being in the forefront was over. At the times that I wish child sexual abuse was not the thing, the scar that he called me to, I remember that Jesus agonized over God's will for him but obeyed. Because he did, the world has hope and a future. What if he wants to take my suffering, my scars, and use them to bring hope and a future to just a few? It will all be worth it.

> He has sent me to bind up the brokenhearted,
> to proclaim freedom for the captive and release
> from darkness for the prisoners. (Isaiah 61:1b
> NIV)

Heart Trouble

I am wired today. No, I'm not wound up or hyper or overcaffeinated. I'm actually wired, connected to a heart monitor. Why? My irregular heartbeat is more irregular than usual. So for twenty-four hours, I am sporting a very fashionable selection of wires attached to my chest with red, green, brown, and black snaps—almost Christmassy.

Prior to placement of this lovely monitor, I underwent an echocardiogram, which is an ultrasound of the heart. The technician, Tim, is a very nice young man. He did my last echocardiogram four years ago. He hasn't changed a bit; wish I could say the same for me. Tim should play poker. He is an expert at not reacting to what he sees or hears on his equipment. I don't know what he thought about it, but I can tell you, it didn't sound anything like a heartbeat—no distinct thump, thump, no gentle swishing. Nope. My heart sounded like an alien conversation from a Star Wars bar scene. I think it was insulting some bug-eyed, six-armed alien and was about to be vaporized.

After leaving the cardiology office, I needed to stop at the post office. My red snap and wire were clearly visible above my shirt's neckline. I hoped the postal employee didn't think I had a bomb strapped to my chest. I just wanted to send a Christmas present to my granddaughter and get out without a SWAT team surrounding the building. The postal employee should also play poker. If he noticed my wiring, he didn't react to it. Unless he was playing it cool while he hit an under-the-counter alert button. But I hurried out before SWAT arrived.

Along with the monitor, I was given a chart to track the time and symptoms if I feel chest pain or shortness of breath. They will compare my chart with the monitor, which will help them diagnose what's happening. This got me thinking (while checking my rearview mirror for the SWAT team), wouldn't it be great if I had another heart monitor—a monitor that would alert me when my spiritual heart is out of whack?

It could beep if my motives are questionable. Maybe it would give me a little jolt when my attitude is bad. When my sarcasm is not funny but hurtful, the little line would jump. I'm pretty good at justifying my motives, attitudes, and quirky personality. (See, I just did it.) But if I got a printout of what my heart was doing during the day, would I be shocked to learn how bad off it is?

But God has already supplied a monitor to test our hearts. Hebrews 4:12 says, "For the word of God is living and active and sharper than any two-edged sword and piercing as far as the division of soul and spirit, of both joints and marrow, and able to judge the thoughts and intentions of the heart" (NASB). So it seems to me, the best way to monitor my heart is to study God's Word daily and talk to him about what changes need to be made to correct my heart problems.

I am confident that at least one of my hearts can be correctly diagnosed and treated. And a healthy heart is a happy heart, which I hear is good medicine, so there is hope for both hearts after all.

Wiggle versus Jiggle

"Never stop wiggling!" No problem here, although it's more of a jiggle than a wiggle. After my five-year-old granddaughter's announcement that my belly is squishy (and accepting that reality for myself), I decided to try a new workout routine. This one guaranteed tight abs and defined muscles. It uses Latin dances to achieve the impossible. While I didn't really believe it would mimic the results of the superexcited, flabby-to-fit women on Facebook, I thought it would be fun and get me moving more than I have been.

The first day, I went through the intro, learning the terms and moves. Let me rephrase, "watching" the moves. My body didn't seem to be able to move Latin-like. I am half Italian. Isn't that close enough to Latin? Nope. I had no rhythm—well, no Latin rhythm. I was moving to the beat of a different drummer, a slower, using-only-one-hand drummer. But there was lots of jiggling, even several seconds after I stopped dancing.

After three weeks, my waist was more than an inch smaller. Success! I still couldn't do all the moves, but I was getting better. And it was fun. I was determined to get better at Latin dance moves without breaking a hip. Small goals turn into accomplished goals after all. And in some ways, I had success right away. The instructor said, "brush your thighs together." Some things come naturally.

Four months into it, I can say that I am able to do almost all the moves, and I still haven't broken a hip. As the instructor yells, "Wiggle those hips. We love wiggling so much. You'll wiggle at the grocery store," I'm still more jiggling than wiggling, not just at the grocery store. But I'm having fun and feeling good about having a daily healthy routine.

I'm not getting any younger. I know I won't always be able to wiggle my hips like this, even though the instructor insists we can "jive for life." She's too young to know better. I am not. I know how much I can't do in my fifties that I could do in my twenties. But I keep pushing myself because I think it's important to be a good steward of everything God gives us, including these lumpy, squishy, less-than-rhythmic bodies.

So I'll keep working at the Latin dances and samba my way to a healthy albeit jiggly body. And someday, I'll get to turn in this body for one that can expertly wiggle to the music of heaven without even a chance of breaking a hip.

> Therefore we do not lose heart, but though our outer person is decaying, yet our inner person is being renewed day by day. (1 Corinthians 4:16 NASB)

Five-year-old Emma: Mom-mom, your belly is squishy.

Eggcellent Memory

I wish I could tell you what has happened to my memory, but I can't remember. It may be on vacation. But I think, rather, it has left for good. I am getting better at saying, "Don't take my word for it." My memory is just not to be trusted.

At the beginning of each week, I hard-boil eggs so my husband can take them to work for breakfast. This should not be a big deal. There should not be a funny story connected to the simple task of boiling eggs. But when your memory has gone on permanent holiday, things happen.

I decided one day that I would boil some eggs while I ate lunch. It seemed so simple. I put the eggs in the water, lit the gas stove's burner, and set the pan to boil. Meanwhile, I made my lunch and sat down to eat it. Perfectly satisfied with my lunch, I prepared to run some errands. Never giving the boiling eggs another thought, I walked right past them to the garage and left the house.

Returning two hours later, a strange odor greeted me. *What is that?* Well, it didn't take long to figure out. The water boiling in the pot had long ago evaporated. The eggs were definitely hard-boiled. But with the continued heating, they had no other option than to become projectiles, bursting from their shells.

Egg confetti landed everywhere. The stove was covered in it. There were bits of it on the range hood, the microwave, every utensil in my tool caddy, and the walls. Then I turned around. Do you know how far egg confetti flies when it explodes?

It sailed over the four-foot-high wall that separated the kitchen from the family room. The sofa under the wall was covered in it. There were bits on the coffee table and the floor. Then I saw the breakfast room, about twelve feet from the stove. It, too, had egg bits on the table and floor and walls. The breakfast room also housed my dog's crate, with my dog in it. We'll never know if the exploding eggs got that far. I asked him, "What happened?" He didn't answer, but he did lick his lips and wag his tail. It occurred to me that I could just let him out, and the cleanup would go a lot quicker.

I took care of the sofa, coffee table, stove, and walls. The dog took care of the floor. (I washed it after he licked up all the pieces of egg. Promise.) It's nice to have a willing helper who will clean up after me and never tell another soul what I did.

Hopefully, my memory will return someday, but it probably has forgotten the way home. I can only hope not to forget the most important things in life—God's love and His Word (and maybe to turn off the stove before leaving the house).

> I will delight in your statutes. I will not forget
> you Word. (Psalm 119:16 ESV)

Six-year-old-Emma's Dad: We watched Chopped this afternoon and during dinner Emma says, "Hmm, you did a good job cooking the rice, and the carrots are good, but you cut them small. The hotdog was good too. The way you cooked it, it was warm, and you could eat with your hand. I think you did a good job, Mom."

Holy Spirit versus Dodge Charger

Some days I wish the Holy Spirit would be as insistent with me as my car is. No matter how hard I try, my car will not allow me to do something stupid—lock the keys inside. Most recently, I learned that I cannot lock them in the trunk either. I tried. Several times.

I was attending a conference. At the end of the first day, I pulled into the hotel parking lot, quite ready to unpack and get some rest. Parking near the front entrance, I hoisted my suitcase, leftover lunch (that I was planning to eat for supper ASAP), laptop, and conference notes out of the trunk. With my purse and laptop hanging from one shoulder, leftovers in the opposite hand, and pulling my suitcase, I made my way to the front desk.

Discouraged doesn't fully describe my mood when I learned that my room was in another building, which I would have to drive to. I dragged everything back out to my car. In an effort to get there as quickly as possible, I threw everything into the trunk. That's when my car took over.

I closed the trunk lid, but it popped open. Thinking I didn't push hard enough, I tried again. *Pop!* What was going on? I pushed it down again even harder. *Pop!* I looked for something blocking the latch, rearranged a few things, and slammed it shut. *Pop!* I slammed it again…and again…and again. *Pop, pop, pop!* Then I looked around for someone filming me. This had to be a joke. Where were the cameras? It was then I noticed my purse in the trunk. Could it be that my trunk wouldn't lock because my key was in my purse?

Retrieving my purse, I tentatively closed the trunk and waited. It stayed closed. Shut the door! My car knew that locking my keys in the trunk was a bad idea. I hate when inanimate objects are smarter than me, but it happens all the time. Between my computer, cell phone, and now my car, I'm not very bright, but I don't need to be. They've got my back.

The problem is, the Holy Spirit doesn't behave like my car. He lets me make bad decisions and do things that cause me grief. Sometimes it's just some little, annoying thing. Other times, it's a bigger, more dramatic thing that has serious consequences. There are times when he does keep me from doing something harmful, and I am very grateful for that. It helps when I am sensitive to his leading. But I often don't take the time to figure out why he seems to be holding me back. I just keep slamming the trunk.

Unlike my car, which doesn't care about me but is simply programmed not to lock the key inside, the Holy Spirit cares about me personally. It matters to him that I grow in my faith, whether that happens through his intervention or allowing me to fall on my face. When I fail, he is there to pick up the pieces and restore my joy. I wouldn't want him to behave like the artificial intelligence all around me. I need his prompting, his care, and his comfort. And I'm thankful that he doesn't always allow me to slam the trunk.

> But the Helper, the Holy Spirit, whom the Father
> will send in my name, he will teach you all things
> and bring to your remembrance all that I have
> said to you. (John 14:26 ESV)

Picking seven-year-old Emma up from day camp in the rain, I put my passenger-side window down so the counselor could see it was me. As she walks Emma to the car under the umbrella, I hear this conversation:

Counselor: Is that your grandmom's car? The black one?
Emma: Yes, it's a really cool car.
Counselor: It is really cool.
Emma: Yeah, not every grandma drives a Charger!

Roller Coaster Love

I am "one of them," one of those people who will wait a little longer so that they can sit in the front seat of the roller coaster. Why? Because it's scarier, which makes the ride even more fun. I'm not a screamer. I'm a laugher. The scarier it is, the more I laugh, which is dangerous at my age. That feeling of cresting the hill and dangling for just a moment before being thrust headlong down to earth is worth a little extra time in line and a few more giggles.

Our first visit with our oldest son's wife-to-be, Becky, included a trip to Hershey Park. We went in the evening. With limited time for rides, we opted to only do roller coasters. She was good with that—one point for Becky. While waiting in line, she suggested we wait a few more turns to get the front car—point number two. On a twin coaster, she spied out the lines and timed our wait so that we got on the first cars of each coaster at the same time—for the win.

I pulled our son aside and said, "Whatever you do, hang on to this girl!" He did. And I'm so glad.

Today I'm having that same feeling of riding in the front of the roller coaster. There has been a long wait. I've been strapped in, slowly climbed the monster hill. It's been eight months since we got in line, when a doctor first said, "I think you may have mitochondrial disease." It's been five months since we stepped aside to wait for the front car, going through every test imaginable. And now, here we are, dangling over the edge, about to get the results of all the testing, time to take a deep breath and brace for the plunge.

Like the first time on a roller coaster, I don't know what to expect. How big a hill is it? How fast will it go? Are there loops and twists? Or is it a straightforward up and down? Does it go backward? Fortunately, I have my husband with me. He is great on roller coasters. Our first time riding the Superman coaster is one we won't forget. My 5'1" frame doesn't sit quite as high as most people. The shoulder harness kind of pinned me so that I couldn't stick my arms out in Superman's flying pose. I looked like a flying T. rex. I had to ask Doug to reach over and push my sunglasses up for me. He did, laughing himself silly.

When our coaster plummets over the edge tomorrow, I expect Doug will hold my hand and explain the medical jargon that I don't understand. The best part is he'll ride this coaster with me to the end. Every loop, every belly-whopping drop, he'll be there, making sure I'm okay. He has been waiting with me in line, talking through every possible twist, and keeping me laughing. I can't imagine being on this ride with anyone else. Whatever lies ahead, we'll face it together, and we will laugh ourselves silly.

> Beloved, let us love one another. For, love is from God and whoever loves has been born of God and knows God. (1 John 4:7 ESV)

"Mom-mom, why are you laughing?"

"I'm laughing because you say things that I don't expect a three-year-old to say. You say things a grown-up would say."

"Yeah, I do that."

* * * * *

I ask five-year-old Emma a question. Her response
starts with, "My hypothesis is…"

* * * * *

Four-year-old Emma: The ant went up the hill. That's a joke. No, it's not, I'm being facetious.

* * * * *

We were out to eat with family, including two-year-old Emma. We were all laughing and having a great time. When I slapped the table laughing, Emma chastised me, "Mom-mom, don't do that, it's inappropriate in a restaurant.

* * * * *

Four-year-old Emma telling me about her art project: "It was a red glitter catastrophe!"

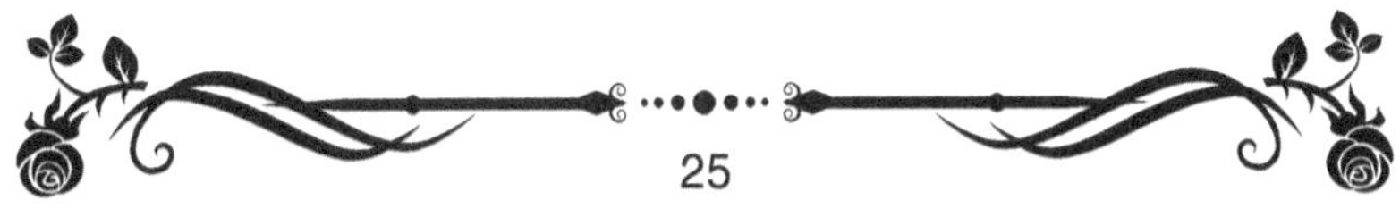

FAMILY

Visiting family in Boston on our way to Maine from Pennsylvania:

> Me: If people from Pennsylvania are called Pennsylvanians,
> and people from Maine are called Mainers, what are
> people from Massachusetts called?
> Five-year-old Adam: Americans.

Sight Unseen

It took a moment for the news to sink in. I had a grandmother. My cousin, sitting at my dining room table, laid out pictures one at a time. "This is your aunt. This is your grandmother." My what?

A few weeks prior to this visit, I had shared my birth mother's name with my cousin. For fifty-three years, I didn't know anything about my birth family. Then the state offered adoptees their original birth certificates for a small fee. There were no promises that names of birth parents would be on them, but it was worth the chance.

I had forgotten I had even sent for it when, six months later, a piece of mail with the official state logo arrived in my mailbox. It didn't jump out at me as I opened the day's mail, and I thought it was probably just a notice to renew my car registration or something like that.

Then I opened it, and goose bumps pushed the hair on my neck straight up as I pulled my birth certificate from the envelope. There it was, my mother's name. There was no father's name, but this was enough; I had my birth mother's name.

My cousin has a genealogy business. She had looked for my birth mother before with no luck. But now she had a name. It didn't take her long to find her. "I have news. I'll come to your house at four." And there we were, looking at pictures of people who looked like me. "Unfortunately, your mother has passed away. But I spoke to your aunt. She told me the whole story and is very interested in meeting you." She set another picture on the table. "And this is your grandmother." *I have a grandmother.* I couldn't believe it.

After two days of processing the pictures and information, I decided to call my aunt. With shaky hands, I dialed her number. She answered, and my mouth went dry. I introduced myself. Her voice quivered, "Oh, honey, I've thought about you and wondered where you were for fifty-three years."

She shared my mother's story with me. My mother was not married and had a four-year-old daughter. There was no way she could afford another child. The decision was made to give me up for adoption, and they never discussed it again. My aunt and my grandmother retired to Florida. Not fond of Pennsylvania's cold weather, I told her, "I am not opposed to visiting Florida this winter." She was thrilled. We made plans to meet.

I was excited and nervous at the same time. Would they accept me? It's one thing to talk on the phone and exchange e-mails yet another to meet face-to-face.

After checking into a hotel and getting some lunch, it was time for meeting #1 with my aunt and uncle. My cousin Joan and my son Jason were with me. As soon as we pulled into their driveway, my uncle appeared on the porch with a big smile on his face. I thought they surely could see my heart pounding. As I approached him, he welcomed me and opened the door. My aunt stood just inside. With tears in her eyes, she gave me a big hug. I heard my uncle say, "When she got out of the car, it could have been Jeannie." That was my birth mother's name.

We had a delightful time looking at pictures and telling stories. Laughter punctuated the conversation. It was a great start to our visit. After supper, we went to the assisted living facility where my grandmother lives. She was excited to meet me. As she turned in her chair to see me, she shook her head and said, "Oh my." For a few seconds, she just stared at me. Then she took my hands in hers and said, "It's my Jeannie." She looked so happy. She echoed my aunt, "I always wondered what happened to that baby. Where was she? Was she all right?" We hugged and then talked about her life and stories of my mother growing up.

The next day, we all went to visit my great-aunt who was ninety-nine. She stared at me for a few seconds too before saying to my grandmother, "That's your Jeannie." We had an amazing time with the two of them—more stories, more laughter. So many times, when I laughed or gestured, they would say, "That's Jeannie."

As I said goodbye to my grandmother that night, she hugged me tight and said, "I love you." At first, I wondered how she could love me; she didn't really know me. But in an instant, I understood why she could say that: I'm her granddaughter. It's the same way I love my grandchildren from the moment I see them. Even before they were born, I loved them.

This visit was the meeting most of us have at the hospital, peering into the nursery, figuring out whose nose she has. My grandmother didn't have that experience, but she often wondered about me, and she loved me. It was easy for her say "I love you" because she has, for fifty-three years, sight unseen.

The nerves have been replaced with a sense of overwhelming blessing. What a gift to have a grandmother and other new family members who love me. Who knows? Maybe there is more blessing to come. They gave me the name of my birth father.

> You created my inmost parts. You wove me together in my mother's womb. How precious are your thoughts for me, God! How vast is the sum of them! (Psalm 139:13, 17 NIV)

Bobbing Along

Every kid should have at least one relative who is slightly off. They make family get-togethers so much more fun. You know, the one who laughs at inappropriate times, plays practical jokes, is completely uninhibited, and is never without a sly smile. They may cause the adult family members to roll their eyes, but to the younger generation, they are saviors from boring family gatherings.

Our family had Great-Aunt Lucy. She was one of ten siblings in her generation and the hands-down favorite of my generation. She was fun with her Philly accent, permanent smile, and adventurous spirit. Her sisters always introduced her as "my sister, Lucy, who never married." That introduction didn't seem to bother her. In fact, she liked the announcement, in case there were any bachelors in the room.

I will always remember the first time she met my then boyfriend. In a lack of judgment on my part, I invited him to a family gathering just a short time into our relationship. What was I thinking?

Three of my great-aunts were sitting together when he arrived. I introduce him to them, and it happened. Aunt Lucy, who had been sipping a high ball, remarked to her sisters (loud enough for the whole room to hear), "He's got nice teeth. Doesn't he have nice teeth?" My whole body flushed, and I stammered an apology to my boyfriend who was laughing and showing more nice teeth. For some reason, he kept coming back and even married me. Aunt Lucy loved him and his teeth.

One of the great aunts had a house at the beach where we all gathered each summer for vacation and family time. It was there that Aunt Lucy and I laughed harder than ever on one particular day when I was about eleven. Of all the great-aunts and uncles, Aunt Lucy was the only one who would go into the ocean past her knees. She loved jumping waves with us. And she was a sight to behold in her brightly flowered bathing cap. But on this day, her bathing cap wasn't the only part of her wardrobe getting attention.

Aunt Lucy was a breast cancer survivor. As a result of her cancer, she wore a prosthetic insert in her bathing suit. We were out in the ocean, jumping waves, running from jellyfish, and having a grand time when we were hit by a huge wave. It sent both of us tumbling head over heels toward the beach, like a couple of Yahtzee dice rolling out of the shaker cup. After regaining our footing, Aunt Lucy was noticeably flatter on one side. The prosthetic was gone. Frantically scanning the water, she spotted it bobbing along on the waves. She pointed in its direction, screaming, "Get it! Get it!"

I was a typical eleven-year-old. There was no way I was touching it. As it rode a wave toward the beach, Aunt Lucy tried to grab it, still screaming, "Get it!" I was screaming too, splashing around it but not touching it. A crowd began to gather, and the lifeguards were looking curiously in our direction. She couldn't catch up to it as it disappeared and reappeared with the wave action. Finally, the bobbing booby washed right up at Aunt Lucy's feet. She snatched it out of the water and, in one swift motion, tucked it back into place.

The two of us collapsed onto the sand, laughing. The crowd that had gathered was trying not to look, giggling as they dispersed. As soon as our own giggles subsided and we could breathe again, Aunt Lucy grabbed my hand and pulled me toward the water. "Come on! Let's do it again."

My great aunt experienced a lot of trials, but her ever-present laugh was contagious, and my generation will never forget her.

> ...from generation to generation, we will recount
> your praise. (Psalm 79:13b ESV)

Happily Doing Marriage Wrong

My husband and I must be doing marriage all wrong. Although we just celebrated thirty-six years of marriage, we don't use the same descriptions of marriage that we hear our friends and even marriage experts using. Words like "hard," "work," "difficult," and "stressful." In fact, we would use words like "easy," "natural," "comfortable," and "soothing."

Just a few weeks ago, while having lunch with friends, those commonly used words came up. The other three couples were talking about how much work marriage is, that it takes hard work to have a long, happy marriage. My husband and I were silent, stealing glances at each other. This hasn't been our experience. What is wrong with us?

Hard work. Really? Obstacle-course races are hard work. Marriage is not an obstacle course. It's more of a three-legged race. The two of you moving as one to win the race. If you fall, you fall together and lean on each other to get back up. The secret is learning to move forward in sync with your partner, matching their stride and speed. And it works best if you have your arms around each other. Once you find the right rhythm, being bound together becomes comfortable. You might even find it difficult to walk on your own once you're untied from each other.

My marriage is so comfortable; it's like sinking into a favorite overstuffed chair. When my husband walks through the door at the end of the day, my body and mind relax. Marriage is difficult because people are selfish. We realized how selfish we are even before we were married and intentionally put the needs of the other first. We show love to each other in small ways over and over, which creates deep ruts in our relationship.

You might think ruts are a bad thing. But when it comes to marriage, it's those ruts that bring stability. When we show love over and over, it becomes a natural way of life, making marriage easy. Did you ever get stuck in a rut? They are hard to get out of. In marriage, that is a good thing if ruts have been forged from repeatedly showing love to your spouse. They are ruts of kindness, patience, humility, trust, joy, and peace. I love the ruts we are in—holding hands everywhere we go, making googly eyes across a room, talking about how great the other is, rubbing each other's tired muscles, hugging often.

My marriage is the least stressful part of my life. I draw strength and peace from my relationship with my husband. He takes the stress out of my days. When I am in a stressful situation, his presence soothes me. One way he does each morning is kneeling beside our bed, taking my hand, and praying for our day, for the needs of friends and family, giving thanks for our marriage, and asking God to strengthen it...every day.

We aren't anything special. We just try each day to love each other as best we can, relying on God to accomplish what we desire. Our marriage hasn't been perfect, but it has come close. I think we'll just keep on doing it wrong.

> No one has ever seen God; if we love one another,
> God abides in us and his love is perfected in us.
> (1 John 4:12 ESV)

Toenail Fungus

"Need anything at the Q Mart?" my husband asked as he grabbed his keys. I rolled my eyes. Really? The Q Mart? You're joking. Although, they do have the best sticky buns around. I could be talked into it.

There are categories of people who go to the weekend-only shopping extravaganza. There are those who love the bargains, especially at the vintage vinyl record store and the used vacuum cleaner place. And there are those who get their fresh meats and produce in the farmer's market section. And then there are the people who go to watch other people. The Q Mart attracts some interesting characters.

I always put myself in the category of "people watcher." But then, one day, I became one of the people others come to watch (and snicker at). It was about two weeks after surgery for a torn rotator cuff. My arm was still in an immobilizer, and I was unable to drive. My stepmother called and said she had some things to get at the Q Mart and asked if I did want to ride along to get out of the house. Sure, I did. I looked forward to counting the teeth of another category of people who frequent the Q Mart. It would be fun.

My stepmother is elderly. She's reached the stage of life where she has no filter and talks really loudly because her hearing aid is not keeping up. The Q Mart is divided into three sections, with two aisles dividing the sections. We started down the first aisle. As we passed a jewelry store, she exclaimed, "What a gaudy necklace. Who would wear such a thing?" I'm sure the proprietor heard her, but it was the Q Mart, so maybe she was used to it. I rolled my eyes and walked on, putting a little distance between us.

We rounded the end and started down the second aisle, her freshly ground beef secured in the cart. As we neared the Minnetonka

Moccasin store, I said, "Do you need new moccasins?" It seemed like an innocent question, but it turned me into one of them—Q Mart fodder for observation by normal people.

She answered, "No. The ones I have are getting a hole in the toe because my toenail fungus is so bad, the nail on my big toe points straight up and is wearing right through. I'll wait to get new ones until I can get the fungus under control."

Wanna get away? The folks around us were a combination of stifling a laugh, disgusted, and nodding knowingly. I'll never be able to show my face in Q Mart again. Actually, I will. People will be looking for me. I wouldn't want to disappoint them.

> For by the grace given to me I say to everyone among you not to think of himself more highly than he ought to think, but to think with sober judgment, each according to the measure of faith that God has assigned. (Romans 12:3 ESV)

Mother-in-Lawing Made Easy

My "miracle baby" was born five years after his middle brother. (Yes, he enjoys being called a miracle.) While pregnant with him, my family and friends thought, for sure, he would be a girl. "She" would be the baby sister to two big brothers. My dad took it to the extreme of wallpapering his room in yellow checks with pink hearts. And my girlfriends made him a pink-and-blue quilt with a matching pillow, complete with pink ruffle.

When he was born and the doctor said, "It's a boy!" I responded, "Thank God." I really wanted another boy—all boys, no girls. I often tell people that it is easier to raise sons and accumulate daughters later, after someone else has gone to the trouble of raising them. I know what I'm talking about. I am a girl, and I know how much trouble I was. I am so blessed with the daughters I have accumulated. They are all gems who treat me like the queen of the family, which I am.

They are not only great daughters but great mothers too. Every time I'm with them, I think they are better moms than I was. They are so patient and calm. They have routines and boundaries, and they stick to them. We did a lot more flying-by-the-seat-of-our-pants parenting. Because of them, I am a grandparent, and I am nailing grandparenting. It is so much better than parenting. It's like parenting with all the fun and none of the pressure. But what about "mother-in-lawing"?

Mother-in-lawing has been an unexpected blessing. I love these girls like they are my own. They aren't just daughters but friends.

Heaven help my boys if they ever hurt one of them. So how can mother-in-lawing be made easy? Here's what I've come up with:

1. Truly love them. I don't just tolerate them because they are married to my sons. I sincerely love them, which means I seek their good, I pray for them, I consider them just as much my family as my sons.

2. Understand and accept that they are my sons' most important people. One of the hardest things for a mom to do is to give her child to someone else. But it is necessary in order to have a good and right relationship with both her son and daughter-in-law. This is where many moms fail. They want the number one position with their son. But that position is meant for his wife.

3. Be an encourager, listener, and cheerleader for my daughters-in-law. It's important not to take sides when I hear of my kids having disputes. If they ask my advice, that advice needs to be objective. Since I know my children (after all, they are a lot like me), I can provide insights to my daughters-in-law that they might not see from their husbands' point of view. Mostly, I can remind them regularly that they are wonderful wives, moms, and people. They can count on me for whatever they need.

4. They don't need to worry about hurting my feelings. I understand the stress of spending time with all their family members. They never have to worry that they didn't call or spend time with me on a special occasion when they needed to be with other family. I will never make them feel guilty. They will always go to their own mom first with a need or to share something. That is not only okay with me; it is right. I get it. I had a mom and a mother-in-law too.

Mother-in-lawing done right is an act of worship, involving love and sacrifice, that pleases God. I'm a mother-in-law, and I love it!

> Therefore, be imitators of God, as beloved children. And walk in love, as Christ loved us and gave himself up for us, a fragrant offering and sacrifice to God. (Ephesians 5:1–2 ESV)

If She Had Lived Her Whole Life

But do not forget this one thing, dear friends:
With the Lord a day is like a thousand years, and
a thousand years are like a day. (2 Peter 3:8 NIV)

My mom could make us laugh, snorting, and all, but she didn't always mean to. She was mostly deaf and would repeat what she thought we said.

"What's wrong with the drapes?" Mom queried.

"I said, 'Do you have any grapes?'" Some of her misheard comments could have landed her a spot on *The Tonight Show*. The best part was that she would laugh too.

But it was one phrase that was her legacy. And it wasn't something she misheard. Although, when I repeated it back to her, she laughed like we so often had. Here's what happened.

I grew up on a quiet street in a small town. Our house was smack dab between my mother's cousin on one end of the block and an uncle on the other end of the block. Forget the "quiet street" part. There were always family members around. Her cousin, my auntie Alma, was my favorite relative. She was really nice to me, and I loved everything about her. She was known for talking a lot and laughing more. She was always put together, hair perfectly coiffed, clothes impeccable.

Auntie Alma owned a boutique dress shop on Main Street. I loved it there. It was something I wished I could do, even now. As a twelve-year-old, I thought it was the coolest thing in the world. She "hired" me to help her around the store—washing windows, sweeping the floor, learning the art of making customers happy.

Auntie Alma knew her customers. She kept a little box with index cards for each one, marked with what style they liked, their sizes, color preferences, upcoming occasions, etc. When a customer came into the store, Auntie Alma would pull out the dresses she bought "just for them."

Her taste was excellent and her salesmanship even better. As her customers pulled back the curtain on the fitting room, Auntie Alma would ooh and ahh and have them twirl, then she would accessorize them. By the time they left the store, they had bought several dresses, along with matching purses, scarves, and jewelry. Auntie Alma was the master.

Unfortunately, I didn't have nearly enough time with her. When I was in high school, Auntie Alma was diagnosed with breast cancer. In only a few weeks, she was gone. We all missed her terribly. And like most families, life events were measured by before or after Auntie Alma died.

One day, driving my mother to the pharmacy after she was prescribed thyroid medication, the measuring rod of Auntie Alma's death was pulled out.

Mom said, "You know, Auntie Alma was on this same medication."

"No, I didn't know that," I answered.

"Yes, she was." Then came the phrase that has become our family's tagline for anyone who has died. Mom said, "She would still be on it, *if she had lived her whole life.*"

I looked at her, thinking she was kidding. Yes, Auntie Alma died in her fifties, but…

I started laughing.

"What? What did I say?" Mom asked, seriously not knowing what was so funny.

"Mom, when someone dies, they did live their whole life." Her brain took a few seconds to process that pearl of wisdom before she burst out laughing. Tears rolled down my face from my squinted-shut eyes. I had to pull the car over until I could see again.

And that's how it happened. Whenever someone talked about a dead relative, it was followed by "if they had lived their whole life."

"Nana would have turned ninety this year, if she had lived her whole life."

"Dad would have bought a party boat, if he had lived his whole life."

"Uncle Joe would have loved this, if he had lived his whole life."

You get the idea. I told this story at my mom's funeral. It got a laugh from most of the mourners, lightening the occasion. But when I said that line, "Auntie Alma would still be on it, if she had lived her whole life." One of my mother's cousins leaned over to another cousin and said in all seriousness, "That's true, she would." It must be genetic.

Not My Way...

"I wouldn't have gone this way." It has become my passenger-seat mantra. When my husband and I go somewhere together, I prefer that he drive. The poor man has started asking me which way he should go just to avoid my trademark comment. Of course it is almost always followed by, "no, no, it's fine. You didn't know there would be so much traffic." The inference is that I *did* know and would have avoided it. I'm just smarter, I guess.

We just returned from vacation: a road trip of six hundred miles and twelve hours each way. While we shared the driving, he did most of it. Seven hours into the trip, we came to a halt in four lanes of stopped traffic. It seemed that it was going to remain that way for some time, so we decided to hop off the highway and go on an adventure.

It was probably the best trip we've done because I wasn't familiar with the roads or area we were driving through. We just looked at the map and took a chance. It was actually fun. I had no idea where exactly we were going, but I was enjoying the ride.

There was so much to discover: quaint downtowns, country lanes, mountain views, even a nudist colony. We laughed that being a nudist in Northern New Hampshire takes commitment. We weren't pushing through as quickly as possible on the highway with only our destination in mind. It wasn't upsetting to stop at a traffic light or meander at a slow speed through a small town. There were new sights to enjoy along the way. And not once did I say, "I wouldn't have gone this way."

For me, this easily translates to my spiritual life. I say God is in control, and I completely trust him. But then he goes the "wrong" way. He takes me down a path I think is a mistake, full of bumps and hazards and dead ends. "I wouldn't have gone this way," I say. Do I think I am smarter than God? I'm not even as smart as my husband. But then I find the path he chose is the best one. When I allow him to drive my life, I can relax in the passenger seat.

Have you ever noticed that when you switch from driver to passenger, you see things you never noticed before? Since you aren't focused on the road ahead and the traffic, you see the beauty along the way. For the first time, you notice the way the trees move in the breeze, the patterns of the hex signs on the barns, a curious gravel path that winds up a hill.

With God in the driver's seat, I don't need to fear the bumps in the road or the unexpected turns. He is in control and always takes the right route.

> He leads me in paths of righteousness for his name's sake. (Psalm 23:3)

Funeral Funnies

It was a sad occasion. My uncle Eddie had died. I drove to my mom's house to pick her up for the funeral. I asked Mom, "Which funeral home are we going to?"

"Simcox, next to St. Stanislaus Church."

"Okay, let's go. It's not polite to be late for a funeral."

We hopped in the car and drove to the funeral home. After finding a parking space in the crowded lot, we got in line to sign the guest book and greet the family. We didn't know any of the other people waiting in line but didn't think anything of it. We weren't familiar with my uncle's friends. Finally, it was our turn to sign the guest book, which we did. Then we turned into the next room and gazed upon the casket with the family on the opposite side.

"Mom, that's not Uncle Eddie," I whispered.

My mom looked around from the casket to the family and back at the casket and burst out laughing. We spun on our heels and practically sprinted out of the funeral home, laughing all the way to the car, embarrassed by our mistake.

I asked Mom, "Why did you think the funeral was at Simcox?"

"Because all the Catholics use Simcox."

"Mom! I can't believe you didn't check."

She just laughed and laughed. "We signed the guest book. Hahaha! What are the chances another funeral would be taking place at the same time?"

Within a few minutes, we arrived at the correct funeral home. They are all pretty close together in our small town. We should have driven around the block a few times because we were still laughing when we got there. Signing the guest book just brought on more giggles. We turned the corner, and Mom said, "There he is." And the next round of giggles spilled out. People whipped their heads around to see who was being so disrespectful. We tried to stifle the giggling, but everyone knows, trying to stop just makes it worse.

We took our seats and tried hard not to laugh through the service. We did everything possible: biting a lip, looking away from each other, thinking about other things. Fortunately, heads bobbing with hands over faces and tears trickling down seemed appropriate for a funeral. I thought it would never end. But the worst was yet to come.

It was time for the most solemn part of the funeral, the burial. We gathered at the cemetery and took our places around the casket. The priest started the ceremony. We thought we finally had ourselves under control. The fresh air and short walk helped, but we were not in the clear.

The priest pulled out a little squirt bottle and proceeded to squirt holy water from where he was standing at the head of the casket down to the other end. As that stream of holy water arced through the air and splattered onto the casket, Mom and I lost our composure, and the giggles started all over again. We had to move away from the crowd. This time, it was bad and at the worst possible moment. We made our way back to my car. We didn't want to upset the family or be disrespectful, but as hard as we tried, we just couldn't stop giggling.

We knew we would have to apologize to my aunt for our behavior. Fortunately, my aunt had a great sense of humor herself. As we relayed the story of showing up at the wrong funeral home and even signing the guest book, my aunt laughed along with us. What a relief that she understood our odd behavior and wasn't angry or offended by our giggling.

In fact, we learned that she had trouble controlling her own giggles during the burial. It turned out that when she got into the funeral home's limo to go to the cemetery, she sat down like you would in the back seat of a regular car. But of course, the backseat in a limo is set back farther in the car. When she sat, she landed on the floor of the car and rolled around a bit, which gave her the giggles. So there we were, at the most somber moment possible, suppressing giggles. We are just a family who finds humor in even the saddest circumstances.

> Even in laughter, the heart may ache, and the end
> of joy may be grief. (Proverbs 14:13)

Love Is a Scrub Brush

I have been blessed beyond measure by having Doug as my husband. He loves me so well! There are lots of ways he shows his love. Sometimes it's the smallest ways that mean the most. Take the case of a long-handled scrub brush to wash dishes. That might not seem like a good way to show one's love for his wife. It's right up there with a vacuum or an iron, not recommended gifts to impress a wife unless the husband is looking for trouble. But in my world, it was the sweetest thing.

We had been visiting our son's family in California. They had a long-handled brush for their dishes. After using it a few times, I said to Doug, "I think this brush is easier for me to use than a dishcloth. My hands don't hurt after doing the dishes with it." I didn't say any more about it. But a few weeks later, upon arriving home from another trip, I found a long-handled brush in my little dishwashing tool bucket. What I saw when I found the brush was that he heard me, and he cared enough to take the time to find one and buy it for me before I got home. (There were beautiful flowers too. He's still a romantic.)

Something so small speaks volumes. Since symptoms of my illness have grown, making my hands weak and painful, Doug has taken on many responsibilities that were once mine. I didn't have to ask him to take on these things; he just saw that I was having trouble and stepped in. That's love.

It's great to have a husband who sees a need in my life and does what he can to meet it. Sometimes he can't do anything but be there with me. He does that. No matter how long his day has been, he takes time every night to rub my feet and legs so that I can sleep better. Most importantly, he prays for me every morning before leaving for work and checks how I'm doing every evening when he gets home. I think that's how he assesses what he'll need to handle each night. These last three years of dealing with my illness have been hard on him. Because he loves me, he hates seeing me in pain. But I am so thankful he has been by my side.

We started out our marriage much the same way. I was in a serious car accident two days before our wedding. The day we were married, I was in pain. There was a moment in our wedding ceremony where we had to kneel. When the time came, I looked at Doug and said, "I may need help." He took my arm and, with eyes full of love, gave the firm support needed to pick me up. He's been doing that ever since.

> Likewise, husbands, live with your wives in an
> understanding way, showing honor to the woman
> as the weaker vessel, since they are heirs with you
> of the grace of life, so that your prayers may not
> be hindered. (1 Peter 3:7 ESV)

The Ghosts of Christmas
Past Come to Dinner

I'm pretty sure my family is like most families. Growing up, we did all the usual holiday stuff—decorating the house with a crèche that included a wise man whose head had been glued back on, putting up a Christmas tree (breaking an ornament or two along the way), hanging a wreath on the front door (and rehanging it every time the door was closed a little too hard), and balancing plastic candles on the windowsills.

We went to the Christmas Eve service and sang "Silent Night" as we switched on our battery-operated candles. I would go to sleep that night with the window candle still burning, casting a warm, quiet glow across my room, as I drifted off to sleep in heavenly peace.

And then Christmas morning came. My mother wouldn't let my sister and me downstairs until she, my grandmother, and great-aunt were ready—teeth brushed and everything. I think they dragged it out as long as possible. My grandmother didn't even have real teeth. That's where the heavenly peace ended. We raced down the stairs, ripping our stockings from where they had been hung with care, then off to the tree, diving into the pile of presents waiting there.

We enjoyed our gifts for a short time before the rest of the family arrived. Then the real chaos ensued. More gifts were exchanged before getting to the biggest event of the day—Christmas dinner.

The ham and sweet potatoes were passed around the table as the conversation reached decibels which threatened to shatter the water glasses. Laughter punctuated the breaks in conversation. Then came the oohs and ahhs over my mother's apple and lemon meringue pies. The ghosts always showed up as we scarfed down pie.

It would start innocently enough. Someone would ask a simple question, "What year did Vince retire?" And that's all it took.

The answer was, "Well, Mary died in '78, and he was still working. And Ike died in '81, and he was retired then. So around '79–'80." Every event in our family's life was marked on the time line of dead relatives. The ghosts naturally brought with them skeletons. And things got interesting. It seemed that each generation remembered events slightly differently, but the ghosts remained the same. And with each passing generation, the ghosts and their stories grew.

My generation was determined not to mark our life events by the deaths of our relatives, but we just can't help it. My son, Jason, was born the year Aunt Edna died. My sister, Lori, got married the year Mom and Aunt Harriet died.

We'll get together this Christmas, and all the ghosts of Christmas past will join us around the dinner table. I can't wait to say, "Mom would be eighty-five this year, if she had lived her whole life." And my sister and cousins will laugh and chime in with their own dead relative events. And we'll all enjoy a little more pie and sweet memories of family ghosts.

Maybe we aren't like most families after all.

> Therefore, since we are surrounded by so great a cloud of witnesses, let us also lay aside every weight, and sin which clings so closely, and let us run with endurance the race that is set before us, looking to Jesus, the founder and perfecter of our faith, who for the joy that was set before him endured the cross, despising the shame, and is seated at the right hand of the throne of God. (Hebrews 12:1–2)

I was babysitting two-year-old Sam. We were having fun playing. As he giggled, I said, "When you're happy, I'm happy, Sam." We went about our day, playing and laughing. Every now and then, he would stop and ask, "Mom-mom, are you happy?"

"Yes, I'm happy," I replied.

"I happy too." He's the sweetest thing!

* * * * *

Five-year-old Emma saw me slice something whitish.

Emma: Mom-mom, are you eating butter?

Me: No, it's a piece of cheese. Do you want one?

Emma: No. (Saddest "no" ever. She was so hoping it was butter and we could have slices of it for snack!)

* * * * *

Seeing four-year-old Emma after she had a stomachache.

Mom-mom: How are you today, Emma?

Emma: I'm fine. My belly doesn't hurt anymore. Now I'm just cute. Yeah, I'm cute.

* * * * *

Three-year-old Emma's latest philosophy,

"I got married. Now the party's over."

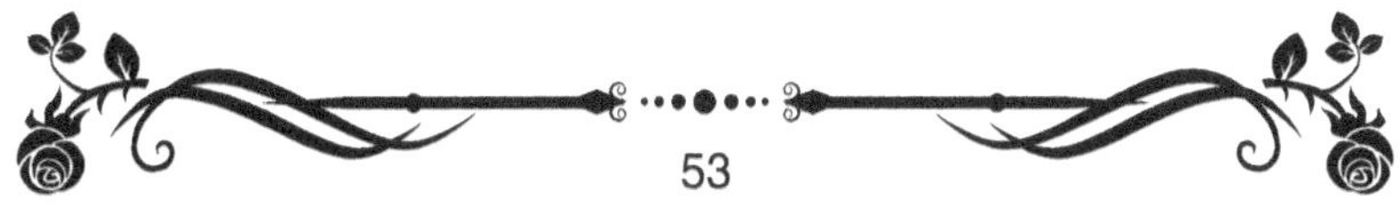

GRANDS

In the time it took me to reset my Facebook password, my six-year-old granddaughter completed two Spanish lessons on her laptop—by herself. I hope I live long enough to see her take over the world.

Mom-mom, That's Me!

I've been called a lot of things in my life: Little Sister, Cici, cousin, Aunt, Mrs. Radcliff, Mom, Sisterchick, ma'am, and some things that I won't print. But my favorite title, hands down, is Mom-mom. When I hear that from one of my little cherubs, my heart melts, especially when it's accompanied by a hug and "I love you."

I have spent the last two weeks in California, meeting our newest grandchild and celebrating her sister's second birthday. The two-year-old usually adds an additional "mom" to my title, making me Mom-mom-mom. But sometimes, she just shortens it to *"Ma!"* That's usually when she wants me to play. Playing with grandchildren is what Mom-moms do best—playing and baking, which can be considered playing, depending on how messy it gets.

No one told me that grandparenting is way better than parenting. It's basically parenting without the stress. Grandparents can swoop in, play, laugh, give them candy, read some books, and wave goodbye, blowing kisses as we drive off. We can do that because our time with the grandkids is just that—time with the grandkids. We don't have to figure out work, laundry, dishes, dusting, library story time, and getting the child to eat their veggies. We've been there, but now we're in a new season.

This is an awesome season of life. I highly recommend it. If you're headed toward grandparent season, don't worry about it. Embrace it. Grandparenting is the best thing ever. I think that's why people don't tell you; they don't want you to know that they are having the time of their lives. I mean, grandparents are old and frail, right? Wrong. Grandchildren do wear us out sometimes, but it's a good kind of worn out, like the feeling of finishing my first 5K, exhausted but thrilled and looking forward to the next one.

"There is a time for everything and a season for every activity under the heavens" (Ecclesiastes 3:1 NIV). It would be great if we could relax and enjoy every season of life. But most seasons don't give us the chance. By the time we realize how great that season was, it's over.

So, I am enjoying every minute, every trip to the park, every pony ride, every chance to jump waves and build sandcastles, every walk collecting treasures, every Dr. Seuss book on my shelf, and even every chorus of "Let It Go" with these precious little ones. Like the autumn leaves, this season will fade all too quickly, so I will thank God every day that I get to be Mom-mom.

Five-year-old Taylor was visiting our Pennsylvania wooded home from her California desert home.

Taylor: Mom-mom, I just saw a unicorn with no horn go into the forest!
Mom-mom: We call them deer around here.

So glad my granddaughter thinks Mom-mom's house is so magical.

A Childlike Faith

Watching my grandchildren wears me out. One particularly tiring day, after putting ten-month-old Sam down for a nap, I suggested to Emma that we take a nap while her brother slept. Emma, being the ripe old age of four, doesn't take naps anymore. But I tried. "Emma, Mom-mom is really sleepy. Why don't we both take a nap?"

"No, I don't want to take a nap."

"But I'm really sleepy, so I'm going to lie down for a little while. You should try to nap too. You can lie on the sofa with me."

I made myself comfy on the chaise section of my sofa and closed my eyes, hoping she would follow suit. But within seconds, I heard her at the other end of the sofa, praying. "Dear God, I love playing with my mom-mom so much. Please make her not so sleepy so we can have more fun together. Amen. Mom-mom, did God answer my prayer?"

Not fair. What am I supposed to say? I can't tell her he's too busy; she already knows that he never sleeps and is never too busy to answer a multitude of prayers at the same time. With a dad who is a pastor, she is beyond her years in understanding doctrinal principles some adults would struggle with.

I couldn't help it; I laughed. And now I can't tell her God's answer was "no" because I am actually not so sleepy anymore. Maybe it was the endorphins released with laughing. But even that is a function God designed our bodies to do, so maybe that's how he woke me up, answering her prayer. Whatever the method, my answer was, "Yes, Emma, God answered your prayer."

"Yea! Let's play!"

I laughed about this for quite a while, then I posted it on Facebook. I'm reasonably sure there are people following my Facebook page just to hear about Emma's antics. I wouldn't want to disappoint them. But the more I thought about it, the more I realized this is exactly the kind of childlike faith we all ought to have. Emma prayed because she truly believed God would answer her. It wasn't her last resort. She didn't try several other things before asking God to intervene. Praying was plan A. And she anticipated a positive outcome, not to mention a quick one. Yes, at some point, she'll learn that God doesn't always answer so quickly. She may need to bring a request to God over and over. But while he may not answer in the way she wants or in the timing she would like, somehow, I don't think Emma will give up.

> Truly I say to you, whoever does not receive the
> kingdom of God like a child, shall not enter it.
> (Mark 10:15 ESV)

How to Spoil a Grandchild

It comes naturally. Precious little ones look at their grandparents with those doe eyes, and anything they want is theirs! We joke that, as grandparents, it is our right to spoil our grandchildren. Our children should just expect it. After all, they were spoiled by our parents. It's our turn. But instead of spoiling them with candy and toys, I suggest we spoil them with time.

My kids had grandparents who did the same thing. Sure, they had candy on hand, but they also had special things to do, games that were only played there, but mostly, they were spending time together. I knew that whenever we asked the grandparents if they could have the kids for the day or overnight, they immediately made sure all of the kids' favorite things were in the house and their favorite games ready. My kids have vivid memories of camping trips, Wiffle ball, and endless games of Hang on Harvey.

The specialness of the time spent with their grandparents was never as obvious to me as the day my three-year-old took off for Grandmom's house…on his own. I didn't have time to read to him, so his three-year-old brilliant brain knew who did have time: Grandmom. He packed his books in a backpack and left.

I was busy making a special dinner for overseas guests and didn't notice that he was missing until I got a call from the Wells Fargo a few blocks away. The gentleman said, "Do you have a son named Nate?" My first thought was that Nate won a $100 CD or something. But no. After I confirmed I did have a son named Nate, the man said, "Well, he's down here in front of our building, trying to cross Broad Street."

"What! Keep him there. I'll be right over." I arrived outside Wells Fargo just after the police. Nate had invoked his right to remain silent. I explained to the officer that I thought he was with his older brothers. They each thought their baby brother was with the other one. We were let go with a warning to pay more attention to his whereabouts. Whew! That day, I looked forward to the time of life that I could drop whatever I was doing to read to my grandchildren. That day is here!

It is my great joy to spend time with my grandchildren. Yes, they know, when they come to our house, there will be candy and chocolate milk. But they also know that they will read books, bake with Mom-mom, and tackle Pop-pop. It's a great season of life, when we can spoil our grandchildren with the gift of time.

As five-year-old Emma and I were baking, I was trying to explain the difference between "good" sugars and "bad" sugars. Licking cake batter from a beater, Emma responds, "Mom-mom, ALL sugar is good sugar."

Oh No, Not Spit Up Again!

With just a few minutes to spare, I was proud of myself for getting ready on time. I grabbed the sweater that went great with my outfit. The sweater was necessary. It was much too cold to wear just the short-sleeved shirt that perfectly matched one of the blues in the sweater. But as I put one arm through and swung it around my back, I caught a whiff of something. It triggered something in my brain. It wasn't a recent memory but a flashback, a thirty-year-old memory. I know that smell. It's the aroma of baby spit-up. It must be on my sweater. Oh no, now what? I don't have time to pick out another outfit.

Don't panic. I have a lot of blue in my wardrobe. There has to be something I can grab. I'm gonna be late. The shirt with the tiny dot…no, too much denim in one outfit. The flannel…no, I've worn that a lot lately. A jacket maybe…nah. I pushed hangers aside—too dressy, too summery, too officey. Ticktock. Wait, that heather blue cardigan with the long front, where did I put it?

In my mind, I am a twenty-something-year-old mom again, rushing around on a Tuesday morning, trying to get to Bible study on time and find something to wear that doesn't reek of spit-up. But the reality is, I'm Mom-mom, the spit-up is compliments of my grandson, and I need to get myself to his house in exactly twenty-five minutes so his mom can get to work on time.

Out the door, I fly, arriving at his house exactly when I'm supposed to be there, which is five minutes after I should be there. I get my instructions and schedule from my daughter-in-law, kiss my granddaughter goodbye, and they are gone. I sit down with Sam, and there's that smell again.

I haven't missed that smell. It's funny that all baby spit-up smells the same. Many of you are smelling it right now, either in person or in your memory. I play with Sam for about an hour, then it's back to mom mode. Pack up the diaper bag, bottle, spit-up cloth, car seat, and my stuff, drag them all to the car, and off we go. I drag it all into the church and settle down for the next hour and a half, hoping Sam doesn't need too much attention, so I can stay in the room and hear the teaching.

He does great, sleeps through the first hour, eats, plays, smiles at the ladies, and then spits up all over my heather blue cardigan, avoiding the area covered by the spit-up cloth with the precision of a trained marksman. I'll try to remember to throw this one right into the wash when I get home.

This seemed easier thirty years ago. It didn't hurt my back as much to haul all their gear. I don't remember grunting and groaning quite so much then. But just like those days came and went in a flash, so will these. They may require a few more chiropractor appointments, but they will be gone too soon nonetheless.

At least the car seats now just snap right into the base in my car. Of course you still have to lift it in with baby aboard. There goes my back again. Oh well, we'll be home in fifteen minutes. I'll drag everything into the house, and by then, it will be time for another bottle. Do I change my sweater before that feeding or wait for the inevitable to happen again?

> My mouth is filled with Your praise and with
> Your glory all day long.
>
> Do not cast me away at the time of my old age;
> do not abandon me when my strength fails.
> (Psalm 78:8–9 NASB)

God's Waiting Room

My three-year-old granddaughter was working the crowd in my physician's waiting room. She was being her adorable self, saying hello to everyone who walked in, dancing to music only she heard, and whispering loud enough for all to hear (on purpose). But like most of us in the waiting room, after a while, she got a little impatient with the wait.

The nurse called another name that didn't belong to me, and Emma said, "Mom-mom, maybe they forgot you're here."

"I'm sure they know I'm here, Emma. It just takes a while sometimes. They'll call us soon. We just have to be patient and listen for my name. But when they call my name, they'll say 'Lisa,' not 'Mom-mom.'"

Emma's eyes grew wide, and she sucked in her breath, "They don't call you Mom-mom?" My fellow "waiters" laughed out loud at her shock and dismay. It may have been the most fun they've had in a waiting room in a long time.

It's been said that we hang out in "God's waiting room" when we are waiting for an answer to prayer. Like most time spent in waiting rooms, we watch the clock, wondering what could be taking so long. Did he forget about me?

Lately, I've been spending time in both waiting rooms, my physician's and God's. As I write this, I am waiting on test results. The tests were done five months ago. Fortunately, I didn't have to remain in my physician's waiting room all that time. But maybe a fresh batch of outdated magazines would have arrived. I have been waiting in God's waiting room. There have been numerous prayers on my behalf—prayers for healing, prayers for doctor's wisdom, prayers for relief from pain, and prayers for clear test results.

As I close in on getting the final test results, I realize that God doesn't really have a waiting room. He doesn't expect us to just sit and wait for him. He expects us to continue to do the works he has prepared for us to do while we wait.

In the last five months, in the midst of prayer and pain, I have continued the work he has given me to do. I am preparing for teaching on the life of Joseph at our ladies' Bible study and for a speaking engagement in the fall on finding joy. I've been working on two committees, developing church policies for child sexual abuse. And I've been writing. I have a novel in the pipeline and a Bible study, plus some devotionals. Also, this fall, I will be restarting a Bible study for sexual abuse survivors. There's a lot to do. I don't have time to sit around waiting.

Do I tell you of all that I'm doing to toot my own horn? No. It's more of a kazoo anyway. I only let you in on what I'm doing to encourage you to continue to use your gifts even if you are in a place of waiting—waiting for results, waiting for direction, waiting for God to answer. Sometimes his answers come when we're engaged in his work.

Many of us found his calling because, while praying and waiting, we also stepped out in faith. Maybe it was a short-term mission's trip that became a call to the mission field. Maybe it was volunteering for VBS and finding you have a gift for teaching children. The opportunities to serve God and others are almost always available to you. If you are asked to do something, don't back out with "I'm waiting on God." That may have been him!

Most of the psalms that implore us to wait on the Lord are referring to waiting for God to deal with our enemies. But even then, the psalmist says to do good, to have no fear, to take courage, to trust God, to learn his ways, to sing his praise, to offer sacrifices with joy (various verses in Psalm 27 and 37 ESV). It doesn't sound like we're to be stuck doing nothing in a waiting room. Listen for God's answers, but while waiting, do his work.

The Perfect Butterfly

Tragedy struck. In mere moments, what had once been beautiful, perfect, was left in ruins. At least that's what my six-year-old granddaughter, Emma, told me. She and her almost-three-year-old brother, Sam, were drawing with sidewalk chalk on my front porch. It was a happy time until Emma realized Sam had scribbled over her butterfly.

"He ruined it! It was perfect. And now look at it!"

I closed my eyes briefly, knowing the meltdown was gathering momentum.

"You can draw another butterfly, Emma," I tried offering a solution.

"I can't. This one was perfect. I'll never be able to draw another one like it. Why do I even have to have a sibling?" (Yes, she used the word "sibling.")

"Oh, Emma, he didn't ruin it on purpose. I think he was trying to add some more color to it and just got a little carried away. But if you drew it once, you can draw it again, maybe even better. That first one can be a practice drawing." I was racking my nonperfectionist brain to help my perfectionist granddaughter.

"It wasn't practice. It was perfect. I don't remember how I did it. I'll never be able to do it again." Emma was inconsolable. I'm sure most of the neighbors knew this by now, but I kept trying. I can't help it. She's a perfectionist, and I'm a fixer.

"It's just chalk, Emma. It wasn't going to last forever. It would be gone in a day or two or the next time it rains, even if Sam hadn't scribbled on it."

"I hate chalk! Why can't chalk be permanent? Then my perfect butterfly would be here forever." Emma's lament went in a new direction. Whoops. I opened that portal, didn't I?

"It's chalk, Emma. It's made to wash away. If it was permanent, you couldn't draw on my porch with it." I tried to bring her back to reality.

"You're just making it worse, Mom-mom. Stop talking," Emma advised. It was good advice. Once a perfectionist has gone outside the lines, there's no eraser big enough to fix the problem. I'll just stop talking and let her get it all out. The neighbors have the option of going indoors.

I walked over to where Sam was sitting, quietly drawing on himself with the chalk. How could he possibly get in trouble for that? Something about the butterfly picture jumped out at me. I probably should have kept it to myself, but sometimes my thoughts come out my mouth before my brain can stop them.

"Emma, you know what? You drew the butterfly in blue, and Sam drew over it in yellow. So I can still see your butterfly clearly under the yellow."

Emma came over to look. She hesitated a second then yelled, "He ruined it!" Here we go again.

As I looked at Emma's butterfly drawing, now smudged from Sam sitting on it, I thought how God has designed and fashioned me and is perfecting me for his purposes. I tend to mess things up and often can't see myself as he does. The ruins I make of my life or the ugly stuff other people pile on will one day be washed away. Fortunately, He is a perfectionist, and his perfect design will eventually shine through.

> And I am sure of this, that he who began a good
> work in you will bring it to completion at the day
> of Jesus Christ. (Philippians 1:6 ESV)

At four years old, Emma has life figured out. She explained it to her baby brother,

"Don't worry, Sam, you won't get in trouble. These aren't our parents, they're our grandparents."

Fearfully and Wonderfully Made

The emotions course through you when you get the call from your child, saying, "We're in labor!" but the baby isn't due for another two months. Excitement, concern, joy, fear—it is quite a roller coaster. And it happened to me not once but twice in the same week!

Monday morning was the first call. I spent the day at the hospital as the staff worked to stop my daughter-in-law's labor. We played cards and watched TV between the nurse's check-ins. The check-ins grew farther apart, along with the contractions. By Monday night, the contractions stopped.

There was relief sprinkled with a little disappointment that we wouldn't see our fifth grandbaby just yet. My daughter-in-law was released Tuesday evening with no restrictions and an appointment for an ultrasound on Friday.

She spent Wednesday at home, resting. But in the middle of the night, the contractions returned. We got the second call at 3:30 a.m., Thursday morning. There was no stopping it this time. Their first baby wouldn't wait for her due date. We needed to get to the hospital. The feelings returned. all of them. This was really happening. What if the baby's lungs weren't strong enough? What other things could happen with a preemie? I was too focused on the scary stuff. My granddaughter was about to be born. It was an exciting time, regardless of the outcome.

As we drove the dark, deserted route to the hospital, I prayed, asking God to prepare our hearts for whatever this birth would bring. Immediately, a peace filled me, not that everything would be fine but that God would be with us through whatever today brought.

We were there less than three hours when Everlee was born—a healthy, beautiful, baby girl. She was bigger than they thought she would be, almost four pounds. And she was perfect. We cried tears of joy, mixed with relief. God gave us a special gift. We were prepared for the worst, but he had another plan, and we were so grateful.

Seeing her for the first time filled my heart with such love. She was so tiny, so precious. She looked like a little doll. I wanted to scoop her up and kiss her, but the NICU has rules. So I stood next to her bassinet and watched her chest rise and fall and took in the incredible detail of her fingers and toes—such small knees. She had blonde hair. I praised God for this little miracle.

Psalm 139:14 (ESV) rang in my ears: "I praise you, for I am fearfully and wonderfully made. Wonderful are your works; my soul knows it very well."

The nurses explained everything that was happening with her and what we should expect. They checked the minuscule IV and feeding tube. They explained the amount of energy she expended just digesting a teaspoon of food. Pooping is even more exhausting. They don't do more than two big things a day because more would be too much for the baby. We could cup her (place our hands on her head and feet) but not hold her or touch her or rub her limbs; it would be too much stimulation. There was so much to learn about being fearfully and wonderfully made.

Every day, this little wonder crushed the benchmarks the NICU nurses were looking for. She was off the CPAP on day two. She was off oxygen on day three, and her parents were able to hold her. She had quadrupled her milk intake. She was breathing on her own and maintaining a normal temperature. She kept on amazing us, being fearfully and wonderfully made.

On day nine, I entered the NICU with my son. He said, "Do you want to hold her?" He opened the side of the Isolette, and I cupped my hands on her head and feet. Then he said, "Why don't you sit down?"

"Because I won't be able to reach her. Remember, I'm short with T. rex arms."

"No, sit down, and you can hold her in your arms."

What! I get to finally cuddle this precious little bundle? I sat myself right down. My son lifted his daughter (which he could have done with one hand but carefully used two) and put her in my arms. I would have cried, but my smile was so big; it made my eyes squint shut, not allowing any tears to escape. It felt like I was only holding the blanket. She was so light and so small and so fearfully and wonderfully made.

Day fourteen, the feeding tube was removed. Day twenty, my son and daughter-in-law stayed overnight in a regular hospital room with the baby, preparing to take her home in the morning. It was my son's birthday—what a gift! All her tests had come back normal. She was perfect. On day twenty-one, they left the hospital as a family. Three weeks. The medical staff had said she might have to stay in the hospital for eight weeks but could go home in three to four weeks if all went perfectly.

Being fearfully and wonderfully made took on a new meaning as I marveled over this beautiful, intricate creation. I will never read that psalm again without thinking of my tiniest granddaughter, so small yet so perfect—fearfully and wonderfully made.

I'm Coming!

A few weeks ago, I had the joy of visiting my west coast granddaughters. During our excursions, my sweet little two-year-old granddaughter would let our destination know we were on our way by announcing, "I'm coming!" As soon as the latch of her car seat was secured, she would say, "I'm coming, SeaWorld!" The closer we got, the more emphatic she got. *"I'm coming, SeaWorld!"* By the time we pulled into the parking lot, I fully expected the dolphins to be applauding our arrival. She's the cutest thing.

It got me thinking of when Jesus said "I'm coming" at the end of the book of Revelation. Like little Taylor's announcement, this one, too, is full of expectation and wonder. And, like hers, his is repeated three times, with the last one sounding a little more emphatic, "Surely I am coming soon."

SeaWorld didn't know Taylor's arrival at their ocean-themed entrance was imminent, even though she was imploring them all along our ten-minute drive there. We, on the other hand, can (and should) be watching and waiting eagerly for Jesus's coming. He didn't wait until the end of the book to tell us he was coming back. Throughout his ministry, he said he would have to leave this world once he paid the debt we owed, but he would come back after preparing a place for us.

> And if I go and prepare a place for you, I will come again and take you to myself, that where I am you may be also. (John 14:3 ESV)

SeaWorld welcomed us through the gates, just like they welcome everyone else. They were happy to see us, but we were nothing special to them, even though we are season ticket holders with a two-year-old who practically dances through the gate. And the child has the power to get her mom-mom to touch sharks! Yet SeaWorld does not recognize her as anything special.

But they were ready for us. They had their smiles on and their cameras ready. The dolphins were warmed up, ready to perform. Everything was set up to guide us to the shark tanks and make sure we passed by or through the themed gift shops at the end of each attraction.

When Jesus comes again, not everyone will be ready for his appearance, but everyone will recognize who he is. For some, it will be that sinking feeling of regret like you never felt before, way more than when the roller coaster starts moving and you think you may have made a mistake. This one is forever. There won't be any mistaking who he is. Stars will be falling from the sky. Trumpets will be blowing. Don't worry; you're not going to miss it, no matter where you are.

But for those who have been waiting and watching for him, their excitement will be overflowing. And they will dance through heaven's gates with great joy—a joy that will last forever.

> He who testifies to these things says, "Surely I am coming soon." Amen. Come, Lord Jesus! (Revelation 22:20 ESV)

Mom-mom: Where should we take Pop-pop for dinner for his birthday?

Emma: I think Domino's.

Mom-mom: I don't think Domino's is one of his favorite restaurants.

Emma: Well, there's another Domino's.

She's not wrong.

* * * * *

Three-year-old Emma: Mom-mom, stop laughing and pay attention.

* * * * *

Four-year-old Taylor: When I was a baby and Mommy played this song, I would shake my booty. I was a crazy baby.

* * * * *

Pop-pop went for a walk with us after work.

Pop-pop: What did you and Mom-mom talk about today, Emma?

Three-year-old Emma: Mom-mom told me about turtles and tortoises.

Pop-pop: Oh really, What did she tell you?

Emma: Mom-mom said that tortoises spend most of their life on the land…blah, blah, blah. And turtles spend most of their life in the water…blah, blah, blah.

I am sure that is exactly what I said.

KIDS

My son and I were talking as we drove home. I pulled up to an intersection. We continued our discussion for several seconds. Then he said, "Mom, aren't you going to go?"

"I was waiting for the light to turn green."

He said, "Stop signs don't usually do that."

I'll have to remember that.

Raising Boys
(or Fights, Football, and Stinky Feet)

In the past few months, a few parents of young boys have asked me the secret to raising boys without losing your mind. I'm not sure I achieved that, but my boys have grown into really wonderful men. That, I think, is what they are really asking about.

It's hard to believe that, one day, their boys, who at the moment are half killing each other, could possibly turn out okay. Most of us aren't trying to raise the next president of the United States. We just want them to stop fighting, stop calling their brother names, and stop making such a mess. These parents just need a little encouragement that this, too, shall pass.

Talking with these parents has caused me to remember the days of having three young boys in the house. There were days (most of them) that it was total chaos. Since we homeschooled, they were with me all day every day. There were always books and papers and toys everywhere. Buzz Lightyear broke the glass on a museum—hung, signed artist print as he was "falling with style." They used whatever they could find to sled down the stairs. And, in case you didn't know, boys' laundry smells bad, really, really bad.

One of the things I remember them doing happened when I thought the older two were mature enough to stay at home alone for a short time. But when I returned home, I saw the glass in the bird feeder was shattered all over the ground. What could have happened? I asked the boys about it.

"How did the bird feeder glass get broken?"

"Jason shot it with the BB gun."

"Why were you shooting at the bird feeder? You know you are not allowed to do any shooting when I'm not home and definitely not from the kitchen window toward the neighbor's house."

"I wasn't shooting at the bird feeder. I was shooting the onion off the top of it and missed," Jason reasoned.

"Why was there an onion on the bird feeder?" I queried.

"Because we didn't have any apples."

"Why were you going to shoot an apple off the bird feeder?"

"Because that was safer than shooting it off Tim's head."

Can't really argue with that. As a creative homeschool mom, the thought went through my mind that this could count as music and history. No, no, I need to use this teachable moment to let them know what they did was very wrong.

"Don't tell your father. Someday, this will be a funny story. Today is not that day."

And that's how we survived boys, not taking anything too seriously and always having each other's back. Sometimes that meant not telling the other parent *everything* that happened in a day. It worked for us. We were always on the same page with discipline and direction for our family. So it was okay if sometimes I didn't know things they did and sometimes Dad didn't know; we were on a "need to know" basis. I don't even like it now when they tell me things they did that I wasn't aware of at the time.

That's how we kept our sanity—well, that and a lot of prayer. We prayed individually, as a couple, and as a family. We didn't do everything right, but we loved each other. I see their cherubic faces when I read in Proverbs that love covers a multitude of sins. I think we had a good balance of overlooking inconsequential wrongs, disciplining when necessary, forgiving quickly, and laughing whenever possible.

So I guess that will be my advice to these frazzled parents. And one more thing, hold the things of this world loosely because they are probably going to get broken.

Before you know it, the boys will be grown and dealing with their own little ones while you relax in the quiet of your empty nest and melt at the faces of your perfect grandchildren who are driving their parents crazy.

> I have no greater joy than this, to hear of my children walking in the truth. (3 John 1:14 NASB)

Seven-year-old Emma: Mom-mom, what are those dark things under
    your eyes?
Me: The circles or the bags?
Emma: Yeah.

Big, Brawny Guardian Angels

I don't know how it happened, but in the process of raising three boys, somehow, we only ended up in the emergency room twice, seeking stitches, once each for child number two and number three. I could be wrong. My memory fails me as frequently as Sonic changes its menu. But I don't think our number one child ever had stitches in an ER. He *is* the only one who rode in an ambulance after a near-death experience but no stitches. (As it turned out, what looked like a deadly sledding accident wasn't nearly as bad as all that.)

Was it good-parenting practices? Did we cover them in bubble wrap? Maybe they never stepped outside or made a wrong move. We were homeschoolers after all. Ha! Maybe it was because their dad was a nurse and didn't feel a need for emergency intervention until body parts were pretty much falling off.

Child number three's injury was a pinky, and he was small, so it only needed one stitch because that's all it could hold. Child number two's injury was a little worse. On the phone call with the emergency room, Dr. Dad asked what plastic surgeon was on call. Before you get worried, it was an elbow, and there just wasn't much skin left.

The boys didn't make it easy. There were baseballs and bats, hockey sticks, pucks, and balls landing on body parts not covered by PPE (not the COVID kind), spills on granite rocks too numerous to count, Rollerblades, Boogie Boards, bikes, projectile toys and sports equipment, even (dare I say) lawn darts. How they survived childhood is anybody's guess. Then they got older and started driving and using axes and chainsaws and power tools but still no ER visits. How could this be?

I don't believe in luck or coincidence. So those were ruled out. I know my boys were not excessively careful. So that's out. I'm sure God had plans for them, which required them to live, but a few stitches now and then wouldn't have changed those plans. So what was it?

Finishing up a class with Dr. Derek Thomas, I think I may have an answer: guardian angels, maybe more than one per child. He was commenting on how God assigns "guardians" to us to bring us "all the way to glory." What a comforting thought. I have joked in the past that some of us need the really big, brawny angels to keep us from harm. Some of us need more than one. I don't know exactly how it works, but I am glad God sends them.

Our boys have made it to adulthood. Number one is a teacher; number two is a pastor; number three is a surgical technician. They are all trained to help people in different ways.

We are about to embark on a family vacation. We may need to employ all their skills with all six grandchildren together. I hope number three can just relax. But should we need him, I've heard good things about his suturing skills. Maybe we can still avoid the ER. And I am also confident that same band of guardians is still on duty, along with another squad, maybe a platoon. Either way, we're in good hands, granite rocks and all.

> He will command His angels concerning you to guard you in all your ways. On their hands they will bear you up, lest you strike your foot against a stone. (Psalm 91:10–11 ESV)

Moms and Sons

There's an old joke that goes: Why did Jesus take the time to fold his grave clothes after he arose? Because he knew his mother was coming to the tomb.

Those of us who have raised boys smile because we get it. The likelihood that one of our sons would leave their pajamas neatly folded on their pillow is every mother's dream, maybe even a measure of parenting success. But okay, Jesus was perfect.

Like some children develop allergies, mine developed a condition that caused their clothing to explode from their bodies when they entered the house, landing on chairs, bannisters, sofas, and floors. I think it had something to do with the change in temperature or barometric pressure. It also caused temporary blindness. They couldn't see where their clothes had landed and, therefore, couldn't pick them up and put them away.

I wonder sometimes what the day-to-day life of raising Jesus was like. Mary probably didn't have to tell him more than once to clean his room or take out the trash. But I bet, in a lot of ways, it was just like mine. And I bet Mary enjoyed a good laugh with her sons. After all, when you're raising boys, laughing goes with the territory.

Did she laugh at their jokes or when a snake showed up in her laundry basket? Did she stop what she was doing to play a game or slide down the stairs with them on their woolen mats, landing in a pile of giggles at the bottom? Did she give them a sideways smile as they snuck something into the house? Did her sons keep her laughing like mine did with me?

A few months ago, I met some members of my birth family. Although my birth mother has passed, and I will never know her, according to family members, I have her laugh. When I laugh, they say it's like having her back again. It's so strange to me. My laugh is the same as the mother I never knew. But what a great thing to have in common. Since she loved to laugh as much as I do, it seems perfect.

The Bible doesn't tell us what Jesus's childhood was like. But I'm sure it was filled with laughter. He came to bring abundant life. I don't think life could be lived abundantly without laughter. The Bible does tell us that a merry heart is good medicine (Proverbs 17:22) and that God puts laughter into our mouths and fills us with joy (Psalm 126). Being the source of our life and joy, it just makes sense that Jesus spent time laughing.

I hope that when I'm gone, my sons remember the times we laughed together, that I didn't spend a lot of time worrying, and was always willing to drop the mundane for a chance to do something fun with them. Of all the things in Proverbs 31 that I could strive for, it is verse 25 (ESV) that is my goal: "Strength and dignity are her clothing, and she laughs at the time to come." Take some time to laugh today.

So Many Beans

Harvest time. Finally. After a summer of cultivating, planting, and weeding, the garden was ready for harvesting. I was excited. My boys—well, their feelings varied. The three of them reminded me of the three bears. The oldest one didn't mind picking beans. The youngest one loved picking beans. And the middle one compared picking beans to the death sentence.

Our garden was not what I would call large. It was about twenty feet long by ten feet wide. Three rows of our garden were occupied by beans, green and yellow. Once they grew to about finger length, it was time to pick. I sent the boys out to the garden with bags in hand. Each one had one row of beans to pick. The oldest and youngest finished their rows, while the middle languished throughout the day.

Several times a day, he limped into the house for water breaks, then lunch, and then snack. Often, great complaints accompanied him. The sun was too hot. There were too many beans. His shoes were getting dirty. His fingers hurt.

Sometime late in the day, he completed his arduous chore of picking one row of beans. As he deposited his bag of beans on the kitchen table, he plopped down in a chair and exclaimed, "I'm gonna die." Pitiful.

Fortunately, our chore-filled weeks often ended with a weekend at his grandparent's house at the beach. One Friday afternoon, as we drove through the Delaware farmland, we passed a field of beans. It was at least a full acre of beans. There was one man walking through the rows of beans. Staring out the window, my empathetic son said, "That poor guy's gotta pick all those beans." His anguish was evident.

He clearly felt for this man, a kindred spirit in the world of bean picking.

I'm sure the poor man did not have to pick all those beans, at least not alone. But I'm glad my boy had empathy for him. It revealed his heart. He genuinely hurt for this man. Of course, he didn't say, "Mom, can we stop and help him?" He was young and worn out from his own week of bean picking. But God was working on his heart. That kind of response would come with time. Although, by then, he would realize that guy didn't have to pick all those beans.

In my mind, forcing my son to complete his chores would teach him important lessons, like perseverance and a good work ethic. But God had more for him. He used the simple act (even though my son made it harder than it was) of picking beans to cultivate a compassionate heart. Isn't it just like God to take something I thought would teach one lesson and use it in a deeper way I never considered?

> For we are His workmanship, created in Christ Jesus for good works, which God prepared beforehand so that we would walk in them. (Ephesians 2:10 NASB)

A Father's Whistle

My husband has magical powers. When our kids were young, Doug whistled, and our children magically appeared. No matter what they were doing or who they were with, when they heard that whistle, they came running. They knew their dad's whistle. They ignored other whistles but not his. Even now, with the boys all grown up with their own children, I'd be willing to bet, if their dad whistled, the boys would at least turn their heads toward him.

I'm not sure how it started. But having three boys, I imagine Doug whistled to get their attention because they were doing something they shouldn't. Shocking, I know. But it was most often used when we were out somewhere, like the Little League Fields, and the boys were scattered all over. One whistle, and our family was reunited and ready to go in a matter of seconds.

I can't whistle. I mean, I can whistle a little bit, but it's mostly air with a slight melodic sound to it. I sound like Wheezy from Toy Story—the little plastic penguin with a worn-out squeaker. My husband's whistle is not weak or squeaky. It's ear piercing, and he does it effortlessly. He has done it automatically, without warning, if he saw that one of the boys needed immediate attention. If I happened to be standing close to him in those moments, my ears would ring for a while. Maybe that explains my poor hearing now, hmm.

My husband hasn't needed to use his whistle in a very long time. It's not that he doesn't whistle at all. His child-calling whistle isn't the only whistle he has. He can imitate almost any bird. He's had long conversations with a number of birds. I don't know what he's saying to them, but I'm pretty sure he invited one of them to move in with us. It built its nest in our dryer exhaust, which required it to enter the outside vent and make two ninety-degree turns to get to the dryer. Doug needs to stop whistling to birds.

As I was doing my daily Bible reading one day, I came across a verse that reminded me of those days when Doug would call the boys with his whistle. God said, "I will whistle for them and gather them in, for I have redeemed them, and they shall be as many as they were before" (Zechariah 10:8 ESV). How cool is that? God, our Abba Father, will call us in with a whistle.

This portion of Zechariah is a prophecy of the end-times. I wonder if that trumpet blast we wait anxiously to hear is God whistling for us. I know how loud my husband's whistle can be, so I'm sure God's whistle could be a trumpet blast that will be heard to the ends of the earth.

I don't know about you, but when my Abba, Father, whistles, I plan to drop everything and run to him. Finally, it will be time to go home, to be gathered in together with all my brothers and sisters to be united with our Father. Our brother, Jesus, promises he will come soon to gather us up with him. I'll be watching the clouds, praying he comes quickly, and listening for that unmistakable whistle.

A Bouncy, Flouncy Cup of Fun

Ever since my two older boys turned eight and eleven, there were two things they were passionate about—playing baseball and raising Seeing Eye® puppies. When raising boys and puppies, things can get messy (and, at times, a little gross). Like most boys, mine were not exactly neat. Their rooms were littered with dirty clothes, toys, shoes, and petrified food. Add puppies into the mix, and there were *chewed* clothes, toys, shoes, and less of the petrified food.

Our first Seeing Eye® puppy was a yellow Labrador retriever named Abbey. She taught us a lot, not just about raising puppies but about the benefits of keeping the house organized, having a schedule, and not dillydallying when it was time to go. We also learned that smart puppies get bored. And when puppies are bored, they get into trouble.

One of the few times my boys cleaned their room, they neatly lined up all their shoes under the bunk bed. Abbey slept on a tie-down next to their bed. During the night, she managed to reach every shoe and chew off the back of each one. Even when the boys were neat and organized, the puppy had the last laugh. Fortunately, the boys kept their baseball cleats in the closet.

No matter how organized we tried to be, it seemed we were always running late. The problem was usually because one of the boys couldn't find a matching uniform sock. But one day, as we were running late for a baseball game, my younger son found all his gear, but Abbey had chewed his athletic cup. He clearly wasn't going to be able to wear it. Having sharp edges on your cup could definitely ruin a boy's game. So I shooed the boys into the car and dropped them at the game then made a beeline for the sporting goods store.

It didn't take long to find what I needed. I was in a hurry to get it to my son before the game started because he wouldn't be allowed to play without it. Rushing at the checkout, I told the cashier not to bother with a bag. I grabbed the molded plastic package and headed for the car. Just as I stepped off the curb, I must have squeezed the package too hard. The cup squirted out into the street—not just any street but the main street through town, filled with five o'clock traffic.

I bolted after it, chasing it around in the zigzag pattern it was making as the oddly shaped rubber-rimmed object bounced this way and that. I wondered if I was on Candid Camera as I darted around in the street, chasing a runaway athletic cup and dodging traffic. It's good I have a sense of humor and love my boys.

The elusive cup took one more crazy bounce and came to rest under my car. Great. I hit the ground and wiggled my body as far under the car as possible. My five-foot-one-inch length and tyrannosaur arms were not ideal for reaching under cars. Finally, with great effort, I was able to snag it. I shimmied out, brushed dirt and asphalt from my clothes, and jumped into the front seat, amazed I was still in one piece (along with the cup). Nine minutes until game time.

Five minutes later, I arrived at the baseball field with the captured cup and sprinted to the dugout. Keeping it in a vicelike grip, I found my son in the dugout and handed over his new cup (a little scuffed). I tried to squelch my giggles, not wanting to draw undue attention to my eight-year-old boy. But I did warn him to be careful putting it in place. It's a rascally little thing.

Watch out for those dogs, those evildoers, those mutilators of the flesh. (Philippians 3:2 NIV)

The Great Mouse Hunt

The peace of a quiet evening at home was shattered as a mouse ran across the family room floor. My scream woke the dogs. The mouse, running right past their noses, did not. My son, Nate, jumped a little from his prone position on the sofa but quickly settled back down. "It's just a mouse," he said.

"Don't just lie there. Get it!" I pulled my feet up onto my chair. "Where did it go?"

"Under the TV stand. There it is! *Eek*!" I moved from sitting in my La-Z-Boy to standing on a dining room chair with the speed and grace of a gazelle with one leg. The mouse ran from under the TV, past the dogs again, around the corner, and into my office. By now the dogs were awake and interested in my standing on a chair but paid no attention to the mouse running past them.

Rusty used to be good at catching mice, but his hearing and eyesight had faded. Akers didn't have a clue about catching anything. Although, if he thought it was a toy, he might go after it.

Nate rolled off the sofa. The mouse poked its head out of the office. I turned my attention to the dogs. "It's taunting you. Go get it. Get the mouse." Nothing but wagging tails and cocked heads with the look of *why is mom standing on a chair?* Nate made his way to the office, stopping every few steps to control his laughter.

"Aw, it's cute."

"It's a rodent. It's not cute. Now do something."

"What do you want me to do?"

"I don't know. Catch it and put it outside or kill it. I don't care. Just get it out of my house."

Nate disappeared upstairs. The mouse stuck it's head out the door again, and seeing that the dogs were still distracted by me, it made a dash for the kitchen. I pointed and screamed, and Akers looked. He saw the mouse running for the kitchen and ran after it. Finally, someone was doing something. Rusty followed along just for the fun of it. Then he caught a whiff of the mouse, and the chase was on. They cornered the mouse under the jelly cupboard.

Nate returned with a BB gun. "You can't shoot at it in the house!"

"Why not?"

"You might break something or damage my antique jelly cupboard."

"Do you want the mouse taken care of or not?" Well, he had a point. Another mark on the antique jelly cupboard would just give it more character.

Just then, the back door opened. My husband, Doug, walked in and surveyed the situation. Akers was greeting him; Rusty didn't hear him, so he remained at his post with his head under the jelly cupboard. I was still standing on the chair, and Nate was lying on the kitchen floor, pointing a gun toward the jelly cupboard. "Let me guess. There's a mouse." My husband is very bright and able to put the pieces together in a snap.

He got down on the floor with Nate. "You're gonna need more light." He grabbed a flashlight and took up his post on the floor, next to the great hunter. *Bang!*

"Got it."

Thank goodness. I climbed down from the chair. Doug pulled the dead mouse from under the jelly cupboard. "Nate, that was a great shot, considering this is the tiniest mouse ever."

"It was bigger before it did all that running around," I assured him.

> Be strong and courageous. Do not fear or be in
> dread of them, for it is the LORD your God who
> goes with you. He will not leave you or forsake
> you. (Deuteronomy 31:6)

Better Than Baseball Season

Ah, April—trees budding, flowers blooming, birds returning to their home parks… Blue Jays to Rogers Centre, Orioles to Camden Yards, Cardinals to Busch Stadium. Yup, it's baseball season.

I am a sports nut. But growing up, I hated baseball. In my opinion, it was the most boring game of all. Then I gave birth to three boys. They all loved baseball, and they were good at it. When our first son started playing Little League, I gave in, bought myself a rule book, and set out to learn the game of baseball. With a little one to cheer on, it didn't take long for me to become a full-fledged baseball mom.

Three years later, the middle boy showed extraordinary, natural ability. From his first day of practice as an eight-year-old, Timmy wanted to be a pitcher. He let his coach know, but his coach had three nine-year-old pitchers, so he kept putting Timmy off with "maybe next practice." Timmy finally wore him down, and after practice one day, the coach gave in. "All right, let's see what you've got." Timmy threw pitch after pitch right to the coach's glove. When they were done, the coach told Timmy he did great, and it was good to know that he had another pitcher if he needed one.

The very next game, Timmy got his chance. After three innings, our three pitchers were all out of the game after each one had hit multiple batters. Our team was down 10–0. With nothing to lose and no other pitchers on the bench, the coach put Timmy in.

He took the mound with the excitement of, well, an eight-year-old about to pitch in his first game. He struck out the first three batters he faced. Then our team started hitting the ball and scoring runs. Over the next two innings, Timmy only allowed one base runner and no runs. The team rallied around Timmy's performance and racked up hit after hit. They were up 13–10, going into the bottom half of the last inning. With just one more out to go to win, Timmy went into his windup and threw for all he was worth. "Strike three!" called the umpire.

His coach ran out onto the field, threw Timmy in the air, then swung him around. It was hard to tell which of them had the bigger smile. From then on, Timmy was a starting pitcher for every team on which he played.

As he got older and bigger, he got better. He developed different pitches and became known for his slider. Even if a batter knew it was coming, they rarely hit it. Usually, they looked silly trying. His first year of high school, Tim pitched for the JV team. They won eight games that season—the eight that Tim pitched. The following year, Tim looked forward to trying out for the varsity team.

The morning of tryouts, Tim woke up early with abdominal pain. He tried self-medicating with a donut and chocolate milk, but, believe it or not, that didn't help. Being the patient boy that he is, he waited until his dad was up and ready to go to the hospital for work to let him know about his problem.

His dad woke me and let me know that he was pretty sure Tim had appendicitis (Dad is an OR nurse). He was taking him to the hospital, and I should come as soon as I was ready. It's nice to have a nurse for a husband and a thoughtful son who holds his emergencies until a decent hour. I arrived at the hospital just after the appendicitis diagnosis was confirmed. He would need surgery right away.

I wondered if Tim remembered what day it was: varsity pitching tryouts. He did. As he laid in the emergency room, awaiting surgery, he realized he would not only miss tryouts, but even if he made the team, he would miss a few weeks of games. He turned to me and said, "I guess God wants me to do something else with my life than baseball." I didn't know it at the time, but it was in that emergency room that God first started calling Tim to the ministry.

Surgery went fine. Tim recovered very quickly and was back on the field in two weeks. Because of his stats and known ability, he was put on the varsity team without trying out. He didn't get a lot of playing time but always shined whenever he was called on to pitch. He was recruited to play for a Division III team in college. Following college, God's call on his life was more evident.

The "what if" question, though, still lingered. What if he had pursued baseball? Could he have made the big leagues? He got an opportunity to find out. Tim went to a major league tryout. While they were impressed with his slider, his fastball didn't quite hit 90 mph. And then there was his age. At twenty-four-years-old, he was too old to take a chance on. If he had had the proper training and coaching, he probably could have been drafted and maybe even made the big leagues. But his time had passed.

In 2017, Tim was ordained as a minister of the gospel in the Bible Fellowship Church. Some might say he missed his chance at the big leagues, but did he really? As his mom, I was always proud of his performance on the mound. But I was truly moved at his ordination service, realizing that God had called him to something very special, much more special than major league baseball.

> Therefore, brothers, be all the more diligent to confirm your calling and election, for if you practice these qualities, you will never fall. (2 Peter 1:10 ESV)

As opening day approaches, Reverend Tim and I will enjoy the crack of the bat, the peanuts, and Cracker Jack, and all that the baseball season has to offer. After all, it is America's pastime (passes the time until football season. Fly, Eagles, fly!).

Three-year-old Sam: Dad, when can I play real baseball?
Thirty-two-year-old Dad: You need to be seven or eight. You're a little
    too young for real baseball.
Sam: And you're too old for real baseball. You can only watch.

FRIENDS

Talking with my favorite fellow quinquagenarians while on vacation together, we discuss a potential problem. Terri comments, "That really throws a monkey at the wrench!" What? The rest of us double over in laughter. Terri has no idea what she said wrong.

"That's not how it goes," laughs Susan. The rest of us can't suck in enough air to speak.

"It's something about a monkey and a wrench," Terri retorts. It sure is. Never a dull moment.

Riding in the car, three-year-old Emma started to tell me a story about our senior pastor, Ron Kohl. She started out calling him Pastor Ron but switched to Pastor Kohl. I thought she was talking about someone else when she changed names, but I couldn't figure it out. "Emma, are you talking about Pastor Beau?"

"No, Mom-mom, Pastor Kohl."

"Who?"

"Mom-mom, Pastor Kohl. You know him. He preaches at out church!"

* * * * *

Three-year-old Taylor had her first taste of a milkshake.

Mom: Do you like it, Taylor?

Taylor shook her head "yes" while still slurping the milky, cold goodness through the straw.

Mom: What does it taste like?

Taylor: It tastes like a snowman.

* * * * *

Seven-year-old Emma: I'm going to say lots of funny things today, so keep your eyes and ears open!

* * * * *

Packing up the grandkids went like this:

Pop-pop: Do you have the noise machine?

Three-year-old Emma: Pop-pop, it's not a noise machine. It's a sound machine.

Pop-pop: Sound Machine was a band back in the day.

Emma: Yeah, WAY back in the day. (There was a face, hand motions, and attitude to go with the words)

We laughed all the way to the car, questioning if she is really only three years old.

Meet My Friend, Laughter

Laughter and I are best friends. Of course, I share her liberally with my other best friends. We recently took her with us on a road trip. The seven of us squeezed into a minivan and took off on an adventure. Our first stop was the Crazy Lady antique store. Of course it was. Laughter insisted on coming into the overly crowded converted house and almost caused a calamity as she bent us over or threw our heads back. She can be trouble sometimes.

We continued on our trip with Laughter leading the way. She was loud all day long. Every now and then, she brought tears to our eyes. Even when we were completely worn out, Laughter just wouldn't stop. As we said our goodbyes, Laughter quieted down but never stopped completely. In fact, she kept me awake longer than I expected as we reminisced about our day together.

Laughter has always lived with me. She was close to my boys growing up. Even if she hadn't been around all day, she showed up at mealtime. Perhaps her favorite activity was our family vacations. It was hard to get Laughter to go to bed, and she often woke us up in the wee hours of the night. Even as I told the boys to go to sleep, I would hear Laughter quietly egging them on. Yes, she can be a troublemaker, but I just can't stay mad at her.

Now Laughter has been introduced to my grandchildren. I love the smiles she puts on their faces. And I love when she joins in my conversations with these precious little ones. My best efforts to keep Laughter quiet when the parents of my grandchildren are not amused by their antics is almost impossible. She just bubbles up and can't always be controlled. Sometimes I have to take her out of the room so the parents can make their point without her interrupting them.

Laughter was introduced to me by my mom. The three of us spent long hours together, even during trials. The day after I had been in a car accident, which was also the day before my wedding, I was having trouble moving. I couldn't bend, so I laid down on the floor to get my shoes out from under the bed. But then, I couldn't get up. I called for my mom to help me. But she and Laughter just joined me on the floor, none of us able to get up until Laughter finally settled down.

Recently, I found out that Laughter was a good friend of my birth mother as well. Not only did they spend a lot of time together, she shared Laughter with her family too. What's really strange is my friend, Laughter, sounds exactly the same as her friend, Laughter. Life is funny, which is why Laughter is such a good friend to have along for the ride.

Perhaps the best thing about Laughter is she introduced me to her friend, Joy. Joy hangs around long after Laughter is gone. She's there no matter what, even when Laughter fails to show up. Joy is a true friend I can count on in any circumstance. But even she is more fun when Laughter joins us. I'm so thankful God has brought both of them into my life!

> For you, O Lord, have made me glad by what
> you have done, I will sing for joy at the works of
> your hands. (Psalm 92:4 NASB)

Say Yes to the Dress, Senior Edition

Three nurses, an author, a church secretary, and a drama teacher walked into a wedding dress shop. If you are thinking, *Is this a joke?* The answer is no. But uncontrolled laughter is about to ensue.

One of the nurses in our group of friends is getting married. You can probably guess; we are not the typical entourage at a wedding dress appointment. In fact, we more closely resemble an entourage found at senior living open houses. But on this special Saturday, we were just like the twenty-somethings of the other entourages. We were giggling, excited about the dresses, the colors, the lace, the sparkly sneakers. We could rock sparkly sneakers. They would be practical for our bunioned feet. Maybe we could bedazzle our own.

And when our bride came out in her first dress, we oohed and ahhed and told her how beautiful she looked. The dress had the perfect shape, pretty train, and just the right amount of bling.

As the matron of honor, I practiced fluffing the train of the gown and getting back up again. The bridesmaid helped me. Quinquagenarians need to practice. Bending down and returning to the upright position without slipping a disc or having a knee go out on you requires practice and maybe premedicating the morning of the wedding. The laughter from our group was unfettered. We were having the time of our lives. And we have it all on video—well, except that our videographer had her phone's camera facing the wrong way and only recorded her coat and some good shots of her feet. But you can hear us laughing, and that is the important part.

The other entourages in the store must have thought we were out of our minds, a bunch of midlifers behaving like a high school cheerleading squad picking out new uniforms. We didn't care. We offered our opinions to the other entourages. I mean, they were young and inexperienced. Between the six of us, we have had six of our own weddings and a dozen of our children's weddings. We know weddings.

But they looked at us like we were not the experts we portrayed ourselves to be. It could have been the giggling about the two-piece wedding dresses. Someday they will tell the story of the crazy old ladies who were there the day they bought their wedding dress.

Although we were sure that the first dress was *the* dress, we had the day full of appointments, so off we went. At our last appointment of the day, our middle-age entourage was beginning to wear down. That last shop didn't have enough chairs, especially with our aging, aching knees having done more than should be expected of them.

We plopped down on steps and shoved mannequins out of the way on platforms to make a place for our tired bodies to rest. More dresses, a few veils, but nothing outdid that first dress. It was time for dinner and debriefing and more wedding planning and plenty more smiles and laughter.

While this was a fun day, it was much more than that. This special friend of ours lost her first husband fifteen years ago. Half of us were together then too. We were vacationing together, having our typical eye-watering-laughter kind of time. Three days into our vacation, her husband had a fatal heart attack. She was suddenly widowed with three children, two in college and was, at that moment, six hundred miles from home. But she was with three of her best friends. And God was there in our midst. We've been together through the toughest of times, which made a day of wedding dress shopping especially joyful.

As my friend tried on beautiful wedding gowns that day, I was reminded of the words of Isaiah 61:3—to bestow on them a crown of beauty instead of ashes, the oil of joy instead of mourning, and a garment of praise instead of a spirit of despair.

On that difficult night fifteen years ago, I stood by her side as she told her children that their father had died and that, while it was hard to see, she was sure it was God's plan. One thing she didn't know was what his future plans would be for her. Now I get to stand by her side and fluff her train, praying my old knees don't let me down, as a new chapter of God's plan for her unfolds. But even if I need a helpful hand, a little laughter among friends is a great way to start a new adventure.

Quinquagenarians in San Diego

It's always a blast when the quinquagenarians get together. But the frivolity is unsurpassed on our epic week-long trips. Our latest adventure took us to San Diego, California. We boarded our flight in cold, dreary Philadelphia with the promise of flowers, flip-flops, and fun.

This trip did not disappoint. Once we were settled into our bayside home away from home, we strategically planned the events for the week. We had a lot of options and ideas: a harbor cruise, La Jolla, Coronado, the desert, Old Town, the zoo, and of course, lots of great food. The trick was plugging them into the days and times that would work best.

We decided to start off with a trip to the desert. San Diego had experienced an unusually wet fall and winter, resulting in the best wildflower viewing in nineteen years. After packing provisions consisting of water, apples, peanut butter, and celery (in case we got lost in the desert), we set our GPS for the Anza-Borrego Desert State Park.

We first saw the mountains we would cross just north of San Diego. Did they have snow on them? Maybe it was just rocks. The foothills were littered with boulders, which we decided could use some boulder holders to keep them in place. We have experience with boulder holders, but that was only a half hour into our two-hour trek. We were definitely going over the big mountains in the distance, and they were definitely covered with snow. This really was going to be an adventure.

We turned onto a road that ran along the bottom of the mountains, and something crossed our path. What was that, a small deer? No, it was a mountain lion! A real, live, not-in-a-zoo mountain lion! As we screamed, "It's a mountain lion!" it stopped on the embankment and turned and looked at us. I imagine it thought all the high-pitched screams were coming from a wounded animal. Unfortunately, we were so excited and busy screaming; no one got a picture of the elusive cat. Satisfied there wasn't an easy meal to be had, it took off up the mountainside.

On we went to a spectacular but harrowing ride up and over the snow-covered mountains, especially for one of us who is afraid of heights. It wasn't much more than four thousand feet to the top and then four thousand feet down. Sweaty palms, irregular heartbeats, and bursting bladders aside, it was no problem. Our bravery was rewarded with a desert covered with wildflowers. And we regaled the park volunteers with tales of our mountain lion encounter. They were very jealous.

But we didn't stop there. We wanted to see "the slot," a section of desert that has narrow passages for about a mile. It's always a different hike because they have three to four earthquakes a day there, which causes shifts in the rocks, ledges, and openings of "the slot." Let me say, they *always* have earthquakes there. It was nothing we were responsible for.

We started our hike and knew immediately that we must be crazy. I am a full-blown claustrophobic. Another friend is not fond of tight spaces. The other two were downright reckless. But quinquagenarians can do anything as long as we work together. "Working" together usually means making each other laugh. The slot was no exception. I wished they had carved a bathroom into the rocks. Just saying, middle-aged women laughing while hiking—you can probably guess the rest.

We made it through our first day, without even needing our provisions and were rewarded with a beautiful sunset at four thousand feet.

I am so thankful for these ladies who help me get through life's ups, downs, and tight spaces with laughter and renewed confidence. They are priceless and precious. And I can't wait for our next adventure!

> As iron sharpens iron, so a man sharpens the countenance of his friend. (Proverbs 27:17 NKJV)

Rerouting

My friends are…different. Each one is unique and has her own quirks, which makes our times together fun and unpredictable. Last week, I went to a conference with one of my friends. I'll use her nickname, Nedge. Although I've known Nedge for over thirty years, I learned something about her last week that I hadn't known before: She is a GPS rebel. Her GPS says, "Turn right," and she says, "Make me." Nedge did the driving on this trip. I won't make that mistake again.

When Nedge offered to drive, I figured that made sense since she is more familiar with where we were going than I am. I thought I'd sit back and enjoy the lovely countryside. But it didn't take long to realize Nedge has an interesting relationship with her GPS. Like any normal person, she entered our destination into her phone's GPS and took off. But from that point on, normal was out the window. She treated the GPS as if it was on a mission to destroy us.

The GPS would say, in its unpretentious voice, "In one thousand feet, turn right." Nedge would respond, "Why would I do that? I don't want to go that way," or "Why is it taking us *that* way?"

"Well, it says there is heavy traffic, so I think it's trying to take us around it."

"There's always traffic on this road. It will be fine."

Meanwhile, the GPS continued to encourage her to turn right at every intersection, all the way through town. Rerouting. Rerouting. Rerouting.

"Nedge, if you know where you're going and are ignoring the GPS, why don't you just turn it off?"

"I like to know how long it will take to get where we're going."

"But if you don't go the way it's taking you, the time it will take to get there is irrelevant."

"Haha. True, but I like to have it on so I can see where we're going."

"Okay. Why are you turning left?"

"I think this is the way to the conference."

"The GPS thinks it's the other way." Rerouting.

"It does? Oh, I would have sworn it's this way." We turned around. Nedge is really good at turning around. Rerouting.

The GPS announced, "In half a mile, turn left." Nedge immediately started her left turn.

"Not here!"

"It says to turn left."

"In a half a mile. Look at the map. You're the little blue arrow."

"I don't use the map. I just look at the top where it tells me which way to turn."

"But if you look at the map portion, you can see exactly which road it wants you to turn onto."

"Oh, I don't do that."

Then I knew my role as copilot. It was to say "not here" at every road we passed after the turning arrow appeared until we reached the right one.

I shook my head each time the GPS rerouted or Nedge turned around. But aren't we, as Christians, just like that? We have an inerrant instruction book, the Bible, to show us our way through life, yet we ignore it. Peter said God has given us everything we need for life and godliness (2 Peter 1:3), yet we take off with our lives and leave God's Word on the shelf. Or worse, we know what it says, and we choose to take a different path. Do we realize that in His presence is fullness of joy (Psalm 16:11)? If so, why do we turn the other way?

If you have been going your own way, ignoring the path God has for you, what are you waiting for? Open your Bible. Discover the way he wants you to go. Reroute!

There is a way that seems right to a man, but its end is the way to death. (Proverbs 14:12 ESV)

Your Word is a lamp to my feet and a light to my path. (Psalm 119:110 ESV)

Driving to church—

Four-year-old Emma: Mommy, you want to chase cars?
Mommy: What? No, I don't want to do that.
Emma: Oh. You want me to drive?

Quinquagenarians Rent a Car

The day had come; my firstborn was getting married…in San Diego, three thousand miles away. To make it even better, two of my besties were coming, not just for the wedding but as my servants to help prepare and serve the rehearsal dinner and handle whatever else I needed.

A short time after we landed in San Diego, our adventure began. We hopped the shuttle to the rental car lot. My husband was in and out of the rental office in minutes. As he loaded our luggage into the trunk of a beautiful, brand-new Dodge Charger, I told him, "Why don't you and Nate go grab a table at Pizza Nova for lunch? And we'll meet you there since I know how to get there, and the girls can't be trusted in a new city with a convertible." It seemed like a simple plan.

Terri and Susan had reserved a Mustang convertible for their week in the city of perpetual sunshine and palm trees. I pictured them driving all over town and up and down the coast, sunglasses on, soaking in the rays, and completely ignoring the time. Who could blame them?

I knew, as soon as I walked into the rental office, that there was a problem. Terri was looking like a previously dormant volcano starting to show signs of an impending explosion, little puffs of smoke exiting her ears. Susan was bracing for the hot lava that was about to cover everything in its path. "What's going on?" I whispered to Susan.

"They don't have the Mustang we reserved." Just as she spoke, the man behind the counter clicked a few keys and announced he found them the car they wanted. Relieved, we walked outside to wait for the Mustang to appear. Instead, a red jeep appeared. Terri said, "That's not a Mustang."

The rental guy said, "It's the same thing." Our eyebrows furrowed and heads cocked. How is a jeep the same as a Mustang? It's red; I'll give you that. But a red jeep cannot be compared to a red sports car. Back to the office. The office guy stared into the abyss of his computer screen and again announced, "Okay, I've got it. It will be right down." We waited outside, and off in the distance, up the hill where the rental cars were parked, we saw a red jeep coming down the ramp. It couldn't be for us. It was. We marched back into the office with a new attitude, and not a good one.

When I lose my niceness, I go by my alter ego name, Yvonne. It was my birth name, so I use it when I need to be tough, mostly with people who are trying to take advantage of me.

The office guy said that the jeep would be better than a convertible Mustang because we could drive it onto the beach. We explained that we weren't interested in driving on the beach. We were interested in driving around town with the top down. Besides, with the three of us, the luggage wouldn't fit in the jeep, which had no trunk. He said to wait outside. You might not believe this, but yes, a third jeep came from the lot and stopped in front of us.

We looked at each other in disbelief. I felt that if my husband had been there, this wouldn't be happening. Just because we were women and quinquagenarians didn't mean we didn't know the difference between a Mustang and a jeep. Yvonne switched places with my other alter ego my kids call me when I've completely lost my senses, Lisafer.

Lisafer took the reins, making Terri's volcano look like a kid's science project. It's amazing anyone survived at all. The next story we got was that they didn't have a Mustang on this lot. The only one they had was on another lot across town. "Okay, we'll wait. Go get it."

Just then, a Mustang pulled into the parking lot. "Wait, we can get that return cleaned up and have it ready for you in a jiffy," said the man who wanted nothing more than to get rid of us. A short time later, the Mustang was ready.

Relieved to finally get going with the car of our dreams, we loaded up our belongings and hopped in the line to check out with the car where they inspect it to document any scratches or damages. As we waited our turn, the guy behind us started honking his horn. What in the world? What was his problem? Terri got out of the driver's seat and walked back to his truck. *Oh no*, I thought, *I hope she's out of lava.* When she returned, she told us that the guy behind us just returned the Mustang we were taking out. He returned it because it wouldn't go over thirty miles an hour. You've got to be kidding.

Lisafer and her minions asked to speak to the manager, which turned out to be a woman. She seemed appalled by our story, especially since we were telling it loudly, in front of the new customers who had just arrived off the shuttle. They looked scared. So did the manager. She assured us we could take another car from the lot, and as soon as they got the Mustang from the other lot, they would deliver it to our house.

We should have asked for her sooner. Lisafer retracted her horns. Terri already had the luggage loaded into a Charger. We gave the manager the address of our rental house and finally left for lunch.

As we relayed the story to my husband and son, they couldn't believe it—three jeeps masquerading as Mustangs. They were proud of us for not caving in. And they felt a little sorry for the manager. Doug and Nate have met Lisafer, and they pity anyone else who makes her acquaintance. A couple hours later, as we relaxed on the balcony of our beautiful house, overlooking the bay, a silver Mustang drove up. Finally, all was well.

> As for those who persist in sin, rebuke them in
> the presence of all, so that the rest may stand in
> fear. (1 Timothy 5:20 ESV)

Foam Glow 5K

What in the world is a Foam Glow 5K? Whatever it is, it shared space in my inbox with a black light run, bubble run, and terrain race. Clearly, they are all 5K races with some crazy twist that the organizers hope will get me to sign up. I mean, who doesn't want to run through massive amounts of bubbles? Maybe they should combine the foam glow and blacklight runs. That could be cool. Real runners might think this kind of gimmicky running is ridiculous. But people like me need a reason to run, something other than being chased by an axe murderer.

I've never done a 5K that was a straight road race, running for the sake of running. There's no way I would pay money just to run. I need the gimmick, something to make it fun. I've run through color bombs, climbed over walls, crawled through mud and under barbed wire, jumped over a firepit to cross the finish line, even brought home the medals. Pro tip: Don't wear your best running shoes for these 5Ks. They are probably going in the trash after the race.

The best part of those races was running with friends. You hardly feel the leg cramps and bursting lungs when you're giggling with friends and helping each other conquer obstacles. We didn't care about technique or bettering our times. We were just there to have fun and complete a 5K covered in color or mud. In fact, we felt more accomplished by the amount of color or mud than our finish times.

I can't run anymore. Part of me is sad about that and part is relieved. I never really liked running. I liked the accomplishment I felt as I met or exceeded personal goals. I liked the feeling of pushing my body beyond what I thought it could do. And of course, I loved the bubbles, color, and mud. The actual running, though, was not "fun." It was hard work. Running through bubbles made it fun. Making an arduous task fun is worth the effort (and the entrance fee) every time.

The Bible often uses running as a picture of the Christian life. We are to run to God, run to win, run and not grow weary, and run unencumbered by sin. Paul says that, because of Christ, we do not run in vain. If Christ did not live and die and rise to save us, then our running would be in vain. There would be nothing to enjoy along the way and nothing to exalt in at the finish line.

But because we do have new life in Christ, we run this race as the best race of all—color, bubbles, crazy terrain, obstacles—all of that and with the help and fellowship of friends running with us. This life is the greatest race we could run, but the finish will be even better. Jesus will be there personally to put the medal around your neck and say, "Well done."

> Do you not know that those who run in a race all run, but *only* one receives the prize? Run in such a way that you may win. (1 Corinthians 9:24 NASB)

Snorkeling with Elvis

It was snorkeling day for the four quinquagenarians on vacation in the Bahamas. After collecting our rental equipment, we were given instructions on its use by Elvis. You're picturing the wrong Elvis. This Elvis was a local. He was young, dark, friendly, helpful, and always smiling. Elvis pointed out where we could snorkel and where we couldn't and sent us off to explore Deadman's Reef. He had one warning: Don't touch the fire coral. Simple enough.

As we swam toward the reef, we were treated to the sights of tiny, brightly colored fish darting around in the shallows. Then the shallows disappeared as the ocean bottom dropped off, and we approached the reef.

Bigger fish swam below us. Two rays, at least five feet across, swam right under me, and I learned it is possible to scream with a snorkel in your mouth. I also learned that people above the water can hear that scream as it pops out the end of the snorkel.

I surfaced quickly to the sound my friend's laughter escaping out the end of her snorkel—not funny. I don't like large sea creatures in my swimming area. Technically, I was in their swimming area. I thought about swimming back to the beach and spending the rest of the day in the safety of a beach chair. But this might be my only chance to snorkel in the Bahamas.

I replaced my snorkel like a big girl and swam off to where my friends were. I figured I should stay close to them in case anything that could eat us came along. I was pretty sure I was a faster swimmer than at least one of them, which secured my safety, as long as I was first to see the danger (which was likely, since I was looking for it).

We must have been out there for a couple of hours when we decided it was time for a break. We swam back to the beach. Elvis had done a great job telling us how to get moving in the water. But he neglected to tell us how to get out. Quinquagenarians attempting to stand and exit the ocean in flippers is not exactly the most graceful sight, but it is very entertaining.

We were helping each other up. Kind of like reeling in a bluefish, there was a lot of splashing, pushing, and pulling. All the laughing didn't help. As Susan tried to stand, she fell backward, landing on a small piece of fire coral. Uh-oh.

There was one rule, and we broke it: Don't touch the fire coral. And now we knew why they called it fire coral. It's not just the bright red color. Any skin that touches it feels like it's on fire. Welp, Susan's derriere was going up in flames. They had a remedy for the burning, some kind of cream.

We found Elvis and told him what happened. He came to the rescue with the magic cream. Susan looked at the young man sheepishly and apologized for sitting on the fire coral and for him having to put the cream on the affected spots. He laughed and said it happens all the time. I pulled out my phone. Susan threatened my life if any pictures were ever "exposed."

"But, Susan, this is a great story. How many people can say they went to the Bahamas and laid on the beach while Elvis rubbed cream on their butt?"

Elvis stifled a chuckle.

"I will throw your phone in the ocean if you take even one picture. This story is not going public."

Too late.

> So may all your enemies perish, O Lord! But your
> friends be like the sun that rises in his might.
> (Judges 5:31 ESV)

Four-year-old Emma is very advanced for her age, especially with reading. I was driving, and from the back seat, I heard, "fifty-eight, fifty-nine, sixty, sixty-one." I eased off the gas. I could just hear what would happen if I got pulled over. "I'm sorry, Officer, I didn't realize how fast I was going."

Emma would offer, "Remember, Mom-mom, you were going sixty-one. I told you."

* * * * *

Two-year-old Sam is playing in another room while I'm busy in the kitchen. He comes to the door and says, "Stay right there" then runs down the hallway. I'm not worried. I'm lying.

* * * * *

While finding a *Daniel Tiger* episode for four-year-old Emma to watch, she says, "Every time I watch *Daniel Tiger*, he asks me to help him with something, and I'm getting tired of it."

* * * * *

Pop-pop: Uncle Nate's birthday is September 12. Do you know what day you were born?

Two-year-old Emma: Yes. On my birthday.

* * * * *

Four-year-old Everlee, sitting on my lap, pats my chest then pats the spare tire around my waist and declares, "Mom-mom, you have lots of boobs."

LIFE LESSONS

Saying goodbye to four-year-old Emma:

> Me: Bye, Emma, have fun tomorrow.
> Emma: Bye, Mom-mom, you have fun tomorrow too. When you fall down, try not to hurt yourself.

This kid knows me so well.

Casting Off Summer

Summer means long days lying in the sun, sipping lemonade, and swimming at the local pool or jumping waves in the ocean or snorkeling at the lake. At least, that's what it meant when I was growing up. But the summer I turned ten years old, I almost missed out on my favorite activities. I needed a cast on my leg from the top of my thigh to my bottom of my ankle. Swimming was out. I was bummed.

But when I went to the doctor's office to get the cast on, he shared some good news. He was going to use a new casting material, fiberglass. (I'm old; it was new when I was ten.) It would be lighter than plaster. But best of all, it could get wet.

In hindsight, I'm sure what he meant by "get wet" and what I understood by "get wet" were very different things. I thought he meant *wet*. I thought he meant I could swim with it on. Now I'm sure he meant it wouldn't melt if it got rained on or bath water splashed on it.

To make matters worse, it seemed like there were no intelligent adults in my life that summer. Strange because I was surrounded by intelligent adults—bankers, engineers, teachers, college graduates. But none of them questioned me when I insisted the doctor said it could get wet, so I was going swimming.

It didn't go too badly at first, just swimming in the pool. It took a long time to dry, but nothing bad happened. Then came a trip to the lake. Yes, I went swimming in the lake *with a cast on my leg*. But my biggest mistake, and when the adults must have had sunstroke or something, I went in the ocean *with a cast on my leg*.

For a week, I swam, jumped waves, laid on the beach, played paddle ball, did all the things a ten-year-old does at the beach. A few days in, my leg inside the cast started getting itchy. Those same sun-stroked adults came up with a plan. We went up to the shops on the boardwalk and bought a back scratcher. Perfect. I could slide it down inside the cast and scratch away. It gave me some relief. But even when the scratcher pulled clumps of sand and sea gunk out of my cast, none of the adults thought to take me to the hospital to have the cast replaced. After all, I only had a few weeks left until it was time to get it off.

The day arrived. I couldn't wait to get this smelly, itchy cast off. The doctor who had put it on was a little concerned when we told him I had done a lot of swimming over the six weeks. He fired up the saw. Fiberglass was tough stuff! Little yellow-green shards flew here and there as he cut through it. (Fiberglass didn't come in cool colors then.) Finally, with one side sliced through, he pried it open. There was silence in the room as the odor of weeks of trapped sea fodder filled our nostrils. The doctor said, "I'll be right back" and left the room.

I looked at my leg. Well, I couldn't really see my leg. It was covered in sand, seaweed, and maybe a baby octopus. The condition of my leg was slowly revealed as we peeled off things that should stay in the ocean. It was a collection of welts and open sores. The doctor returned to the room with a blue ribbon, my award for having the ugliest cast he had ever seen.

It wasn't until I became an adult that it occurred to me that the cast could have been replaced. Why didn't someone, anyone, in my life suggest that? I don't know. When I asked my mom. She just laughed, and said, "I never thought of that." Really? I guess it was because a doctor said "six weeks in a cast." It was an era when you didn't questioned doctors. It might have been good to question what he meant by "wet."

Of course, there is a spiritual lesson to be learned. Actually, more than one. There is "question everything," "let's do a word study," or "ask for wisdom." But the one I want to focus on is how that cast was a picture of what my spiritual life sometimes looks like. I ignore things that are hurting me spiritually, maybe the amount of time I spend watching mindless TV shows or other forms of entertainment, or maybe I harbor anger or resentment and let it grow into bitterness. And I don't always cut off the hurtful things before they do serious damage. I let the ugly stuff fester instead of getting it out of my life.

I need to use the wisdom God has given me and ask, "What's the problem, and how can I change?" And then I need to be willing to make the changes required. I am thankful that my Father knows exactly what to do and has the power to change my heart, if I would only ask him.

> For my iniquities have gone over my head; like a heavy burden they are too heavy for me. My wounds stink and fester because of my foolishness. But for you, O Lord, do I wait. It is you, O Lord my God, who will answer. (Psalm 38:4–5, 15 ESV)

Split Second

There's a split second when you realize you're about to hit another car. A friend's accident this week reminded me of the accidents I've been involved in and that terrifying moment before impact.

Thirty-five years ago, I was headed home, delighted that my workweek was over. In just two days, I would become Mrs. Douglas Radcliff. As I left work, I looked forward to celebrating Doug's parents' anniversary with a special dinner and then picking up the tuxedos for our wedding. The day I had dreamed about was almost here. And then it happened.

As I neared the intersection, there was no need to slow down through the green light. But the oncoming car, who was waiting to turn left, decided not to wait any longer. He started his turn just as I entered the intersection, and that was the moment I knew we were going to collide. I closed my eyes. *Bam*! The impact was intense.

My initial reaction was to check my face in the mirror. No cuts. Great, the wedding pictures will be fine. Then I took inventory of the rest of my body. My knee was bleeding. That was okay; no one would see my knee under my wedding gown. Everything else seemed to be okay, but pain was creeping into my neck, back, and hip.

I was wondering if I would be able to walk down the aisle. A knock on my window jarred me out of my wedding worries. I rolled down the window. A woman said, "I know CPR."

"Great," I replied, "I'll let you know if I stop breathing."

Sirens grew closer. A police officer and EMT were soon prying my car door open. Miss EMT looked me over and asked a few questions. Then she said, "I'm going to cut off your pantyhose."

I complained, "But they're my favorite pair."

She looked a little confused. "They have a hole and blood on them."

Some EMTs have no sense of humor. She checked me for head trauma. I'm sure she was thinking it was shock. But I was so relieved that I wasn't seriously hurt; my sense of humor wasn't even bruised.

The first ambulance had a backboard that didn't fit into the contoured seats of my car. The second ambulance had a bendable backboard and a giant EMT who could wield it all by himself. As he secured me to it, I said, "I knew I should have lost some weight before the wedding." He effortlessly lifted my 110 pounds out of the car and said, "You're as light as a feather." It seemed I was.

Once loaded into the ambulance, I stated more than asked, "You're gonna turn the siren on, right?" Giant EMT looked at me quizzically. I explained, "I don't expect to ride in an ambulance again, so I'd like to do it with the siren on." He laughed and told the driver, "She won't be happy until the siren is blaring." The driver obliged.

Then the question came that would punctuate that day, "What day is today?" I know they were just testing my brain function, but it got old pretty quickly. It was a constant reminder of all I was missing out on, not to mention that I didn't trust my groomsmen to pick up their tuxes without me. I was sure I'd see jackets that were too tight or pants too short at my wedding. I can be a bit of a control freak. My answer was not the day or the date. My answer was always, "It's two days before my wedding, and I don't have time for this."

Unfortunately, that was not my one and only ride in an ambulance and not my only car accident. It was also not the only time an EMT said to me, "If you hadn't been wearing your seat belt, we wouldn't be having a conversation right now. I'd be calling the coroner."

Some were not as serious. I want to mention that none were my fault. But all had that one thing in common: I knew for a split second that I was going to be hit, and it was going to hurt. One minute I was driving along, happily anticipating the evening's events, and the next, there was pain and debris, my plans ruined right along with my car.

But by God's grace, my life has gone on without lasting injury. I don't know why God allows these things—things that seem to just take up my time and create headaches, both physically and in working with insurance and finding a new car. But I know he has a purpose in everything, maybe to teach us what is important, maybe to help us better understand and minister to someone else. I remember at the time of that accident, I was studying and meditating on giving thanks in everything and having joy in trials. Maybe God was giving me an object lesson. I learn better from hands-on experience.

One thing I do know, if the outcome had been different, if they had called the coroner, that split second of fearful impact would have immediately been followed by the most glorious moment anyone could dream of: being in the presence of Jesus. Plans will be forgotten. Missing out on something won't enter my mind. I wonder if I'll know it right away or if it will take a second to sink in. I don't know.

Whether death happens suddenly or if I can see it coming for a long time, the joy of that split second of realization that I am with Jesus will be overwhelming. I look forward to it. But for now, I am content and thankful to remain in this life, preferably siren-free.

> In a moment, in the twinkling of an eye, at the
> last trumpet; for the trumpet will sound, and the
> dead will be raised imperishable, and we will be
> changed. (1 Corinthians 15:52 NASB)

Desperately Dumpster Diving

It was a perfect weekend for a trip to the Delaware shore with a couple dozen of our favorite teenagers. The weather was perfect, and the kids had a great time together. Now it was time to pack up—just one more trip to the beach. They piled into the minibus and two vans with towels on their shoulders and smiles on their faces. Coleader, Terri, and I stayed behind to clean up.

We cleaned the house, gathered up lost items, and packed the car. At the time, I drove an Oldsmobile Custom Cruiser, the biggest station wagon on the market. It could hold a bunch of kids and their belongings. In fact, it was so long; it didn't fit into an automatic car wash. We loaded whatever was left behind, and finally, two big black trash bags of garbage were squished into the *way* back.

Before meeting the gang at the beach, we had to drop off the trash at the transfer station. We pulled down the long lane and up to three dumpsters, each one with a number on the side. We asked a fellow "dumpee" if it mattered which dumpster we used. His response was, "Which one did the girl at the booth tell you to use?" I said, "Oh, there was someone in that booth I whizzed past?" I turned around to find booth girl annoyingly pointing to dumpster #1. Oops.

I opened the tailgate, grabbed a bag of trash, and heaved it into dumpster #1. Terri grabbed another black trash bag and added it to the designated dumpster. We headed back to the car, and she pulled out another black trash bag. I said, "What's that?"

"Trash"

"But there were only two bags of trash."

Sniff. "This is definitely trash."

"Then what did we throw away?"

Terri started walking back to the dumpster to retrieve whatever it was we had thrown in. Just then, booth girl hit the trash compactor button. My heart sank at the sound of the compactor motor, followed by the crunching of the dumpster's contents.

Terri stopped in her tracks, turned toward the booth, then back toward the dumpster—booth, dumpster, booth, dumpster. She was swiveling back and forth but going nowhere. I spun toward booth girl, waving my arms and pleading with her to stop the compactor.

The compactor sounds stopped. Booth girl bewilderedly exited her booth and asked, "What's the problem?"

I responded, "We threw something in the dumpster that isn't trash." Looking past me, she said, "What is she doing?" I turned to see Terri climbing up the side of the dumpster. Uh-oh. Booth girl and I ran to the dumpster just as Terri hoisted herself over the edge. Booth girl yelled, "You don't want to do that!"

"I have to!" came the asthma-choked response.

Terri started sorting through the trash, checking each large black bag. Nothing. Finally, she reached the compactor area. Ripping open the bag wedged into the machine, she pulled out clothing that we knew belonged to one of our fellow leaders. Oh no.

Bracing her foot on the compactor, she pulled with all her might, and the compactor released its grip on a sleeping bag. Though she pulled and wriggled, the pillow was too far in to come free. Booth girl and I begged her to give up. We reasoned that we had saved everything but the pillow. We could buy him a new one. It shouldn't take this much convincing to get someone out of a dumpster.

Accepting that it was a loss and realizing just how disgusting the smell was all around her, Terri scrambled out of the dumpster. "Do you have somewhere I could clean up?" she asked booth girl.

"No," was her curt response.

"Seriously?"

"I have some cleaner in the booth."

"All right, that'll have to do." We followed her to her booth and used some all-purpose cleaner and paper towels, doing the best we could. At least it would kill any germs. We thanked booth girl and turned to leave. To our surprise, we were greeted by a long line of cars waiting to exit. We looked at them curiously and asked the man in the first car, "Can we help you?"

He said, "We were just wondering what you ladies are doing?"

I wanted to say that we were training for the Olympic dumpster diving team, but instead, I just responded, "We're from out of state." And we nonchalantly walked back to our car.

Happy we could provide entertainment for the locals and smelling like a combo of rotten apples and lemon-scented ammonia, we laughed ourselves silly down the lane and to the beach.

Lesson learned: Do not pack your things in trash bags and take a good look at who you are leaving in charge. Oh, and do not ever laugh hysterically when telling the story to the person who lost their favorite pillow—not ever.

> …protect that which has been entrusted to you…
> (1 Timothy 6:20 NASB)

Stepping into Trouble

Some of my favorite childhood memories involve singing in our church's junior choir. I loved to sing, but it wasn't just the singing I loved. Saturday morning practice was a time to be with friends, and we engaged in as much fun and shenanigans as we could get away with (not much has changed at choir practice).

Since I was the shortest choir member, I was assigned the shortest choir gown. Even so, it was a little long for me. Most gowns hit just below the knees or midcalf. Mine was more formal, almost floor length. To avoid the spectacle of forty kids tripping up the four steps at the front of the church, our director taught us to gather the front of our gowns in one hand and lift them a little as we approached the steps.

But one day, I didn't lift my gown quite high enough. As I negotiated the first step, my foot caught the hem of my gown. But I couldn't just stop. Someone might notice my misstep. I figured, if I went up the next step with the left foot, the right foot would release the gown, and all would be well.

Unfortunately, my left foot caught more of the gown. It pulled on my neck, bending me slightly forward. Another step, more gown went under my feet, more bending. There was no way to get it out from under my feet. But I had to keep going. There was only one more step. Then I would be on flat ground and could fix the problem.

But that last step was too much. I had nowhere to go but down. Hard. After rolling around for a few seconds, I was able to unhitch my feet from the gown. With a little help from the director, I popped back up and took my seat in the pew, hoping no one noticed.

Of course, everyone noticed. It was hard not to with a kid on the elevated chancel area, rolling around in a bright red gown. At least, being the shortest, I was at the back of the line with only the director behind me, so there wasn't a domino effect. I tried not to make eye contact with any of the other choir kids. But I knew they were laughing. Our director, sitting next to me, was trying to stifle her giggles, but she was struggling.

You better believe when we got up to sing, I hoisted that gown high enough to make it impossible for my foot to catch any of it. From that day on, I always overgathered my gown when going up or down steps. I still do it when I'm wearing a longish dress. Thankfully, our choir doesn't wear gowns anymore. At my age, I'd break a hip rolling around on the platform.

At times, we don't realize how much trouble we're in until it's too late. But sometimes, even when we know we've made a mistake or sinned, we keep going, thinking we can fix it ourselves. Maybe it's not something sinful. Maybe it's something like depression or anxiety or some fear that paralyzes us. Things tend to have a snowball effect, and soon we're in too deep to get back on our feet.

Most of us have to come to the end of ourselves before we stop destructive behavior and make a change. God is always there, waiting for us to give up our feeble attempts to make things right and extending his mercy and grace.

God also gives us friends, counselors, and doctors when what is affecting us is beyond our control. These, too, are expressions of his mercy and grace. When we fall, no matter how hard we land, we are never alone in our struggles. Maybe we need to just stop and ask for help.

> I waited patiently for the Lord; He turned to me and heard my cry. He lifted me out of the slimy pit, out of the mud and mire; He set my feet on a rock and gave me a firm place to stand. He put a new song in my mouth, a hymn of praise to our God. Many will see and fear the Lord and put their trust in Him. (Psalm 40:1–3 NIV)

I wore capri-length pants today.

Five-year-old Emma: Mom-mom, you must be getting very tall. Your
legs are sticking way out of your pants.

Lesson from the Blizzard of '96

A blizzard was bearing down on the east coast. My family was busy preparing. Our three boys packed up and fled to a friend's farm to ride it out and have a little fun in the snow. As a nurse, my husband planned to stay at the hospital in case of emergencies. And me? I was blissfully unaware of anything going on at home in Pennsylvania.

Three days before, I flew out of Philadelphia International Airport for a conference in Chicago. There had been no mention of a potential storm before I left. I had checked in at home a couple of times. My husband said they were going to get a snowstorm, but it shouldn't be a big deal. In Chicago, nothing was out of the ordinary, until we tried to leave.

When we arrived at O'Hare for our return flight, there were some delays, some cancellations. But our flight was still "on time." The frenzy among travelers was the first alert that something extraordinary was happening back home. Our flight was canceled just before the entire board switched from delayed to canceled.

Realizing hotels would soon be overwhelmed, our party of four women sprinted to the nearest bank of phones, hurdling suitcases, leaving the more refined business travelers in our wake. We had no pride, didn't care about appearing dignified, just did what had to be done to avoid sleeping at the airport.

We each commandeered a phone and went to work. I found a room at a Hampton Inn, one of the last available in the city. Snapping my fingers to get the attention of our group, I nodded affirmation, and we all hung up, wishing the next stranded traveler in line good luck.

We grabbed the airport shuttle to our hotel and switched on the TV. Now that the city was overrun with angry east coasters, and O'Hare had turned into a makeshift Holiday Inn, the far-off blizzard was a news story. Then they showed what was happening back home. They were calling it "the storm of the century." I called my husband to let him know I wouldn't be coming home for a few days. He wasn't surprised but assured me the boys were having fun with their friends and would be safe there. He was going to stay at the hospital for a few days in case he was needed.

I spent the next four days away from the storm. The weather was lovely in Chicago, sunny and cold, perfect for sightseeing in the windy city in January.

We called the home office of our company and were invited to come have lunch there and tour the plant. They sent a long, black limo for us. We were treated like royalty. The limo driver was friendly and informative.

On our way back to the hotel, he said, "You have me for the rest of the day. Is there somewhere you'd like to go?" We explained that we were only planning to be in Chicago for three days, but now it looked like we would be there twice that long. We needed some "essentials." He offered to drive us to Target.

The limo pulled up to the front of Target. We waited for our driver to let us out, and off we went. We found the things we needed and regrouped back at the entrance. Our limo appeared within seconds.

The driver hopped out, opened our door, and we all piled into the cavernous interior. The driver took his seat behind the wheel and couldn't hide his laugher. He said, "I just have to tell you what happened. After I dropped you off, I pulled over to the side to wait. The look on the faces of people in the parking lot was priceless. Some of them were on their way out but turned around and went back into Target. I'm sure they thought you were celebrities."

I said, "That explains the very strange looks from people in the store. Who but a celebrity would take a limo to Target to buy underwear?" We all got a good laugh as we continued our celebrity tour of Chicago, while our families dug out from under three feet of snow.

Four days later, we returned home. Landing at the airport, it was hard to tell that there had been a blizzard. There was more snow at the car park but not incredible amounts of snow. Driving home, the roads were clear and dry. The farther north and west we went, the more snow we found. Driving through my small town, the snow was piled so high that I couldn't see around the corners at intersections. Day four post-blizzard, we had electricity, the streets were clear, the sidewalks shoveled, and our boys had returned home (via snowmobile). Other than the fact that there was snow that dwarfed my two-year-old, everything was normal.

My experience with the Blizzard of '96 made me wonder how often my friends and family members may be going through difficult storms of life, but I am unaware. In my world, everything is sunny and worry-free, and from my perspective, their lives are the same. It challenged me to be more in tune with the needs of those around me, to keep a keen eye on the storm clouds gathering over them. I committed to offer a helping hand, pray with them as the storm swirls, or just be present in their time of need—much like Jesus does for me.

> Do nothing from selfish ambition or conceit, but in humility count others more significant than yourselves. Let each of you look not only to his own interests, but also to the interests of others. Have this mind among yourselves, which is yours in Christ Jesus. (Philippians 2:3–5 ESV)

Yué's Walk

I needed to get my steps in before the day became unbearably hot. Gathering all the necessary gear—water, phone, pedometer, poop bag, leash—where is Yué's leash? In the playroom, of course, there's a two-year-old running amok, displacing everything. Out the door we went, stopping ten feet from the front door to poop—the dog, that is.

My professional dog colleagues would describe Yué as having "poor composition." The rest of you would say, "She ain't right." Both are accurate. Regardless of how you feel about pit bulls, this pit mix doesn't look particularly friendly. She is, but it's that composition/not right thing that would give you pause. Is she snarling? Nope, her lip is just stuck in her teeth on one side.

She has been staying with us for the last ten days, along with my son, his wife, and the two littles while some work is being done on their home. It's been fun, and I have a walking buddy. So we hit the pavement and are walking briskly up the first hill. I see a woman walking briskly down the hill. She has a definite advantage at moving briskly. I position myself on the right side of the sidewalk. This puts Yué between us. I know you're thinking, *Well, that was dumb. Why didn't you put the dog on your right side?* There's a simple explanation—habit, not the nun kind.

After twenty-plus years of walking Seeing Eye® puppies only on the left, I still walk dogs, all dogs, on the left. Yué is in no way, shape, or form a service dog. Service dogs are smart. Yué's not only a few fries short of a Happy Meal, what fries she has are a little undercooked. But she's family.

So we're walking. She's on my left, and there are small trees on my right, giving me nowhere to go. The lady coming toward us has choices. She can move into the grass between the sidewalk and the curb, or she can step into the street.

I realize too late that Downhill Walking Briskly Lady is not going to yield an inch. I have no time to get Yué into the street without taking out DWBL. Sidebar—I don't care if you are the dog whisperer himself, if you are approaching a dog you don't know, you ought to give him some room, not to mention the fact that this woman doesn't know me. She has no idea if I can handle this weird-looking Pit-mutt, straining at her leash, making throaty, gasping sounds. I'm not too sure myself.

I've got Yué on a nice, short leash right next to me, so the worst I hope will happen is this woman will get slimed. But it's her own fault. So we make the pass. Yué slimes her. (She's lucky we just started out. If this had been a mile in, Yué would have worked up a good lather, which she likes to fling, splattering everything in its wake, and landing in an elegant circle encompassing her head.) I say, "No, Yué." We get a few steps farther, and I say, "Good girl, Yué." A smarter dog might wonder if it was corrected or praised. Trust me, this dog doesn't care.

Some things to remember when you come across an unfamiliar dog or dog walker:

1. Give them extra room.
2. Ask from a distance if the dog is friendly and *if* you can approach it.
3. Assume the person handling the dog really can't handle the dog, and refer to #1.
4. Never, ever, allow yourself, your children, or your dog distract or interfere with a real service dog.

Magic Eraser

I had a dark spot on my bathroom floor. It had been there for a long time. I tried every type of cleaner to remove it with no success. I'm sure the spot is from dirt being trapped in the overspray of my hairspray. I kept trying different things, but nothing took it away. Then one day, I was using a Magic Eraser to get a scuff off a wall and thought, *I wonder if this would work on the bathroom floor.*

I marched upstairs and a few minutes later, ta-da! The spot was gone. As I returned the Magic Eraser to its box, I looked for an explanation as to how it works. Nothing. The box doesn't say what it's made of or what is in it. There's no clue as to why it can erase stains that other cleaners cannot. It doesn't look like anything special, just a white spongy thing with no odor, no suds—hmm, nothing but magic.

Wouldn't it be nice if there was a Magic Eraser for life? How great would it be if you could magically erase the fifty-plus years of mistakes, regrets, wrongs, hurtful words, and broken heart moments of your life? You could start fresh, as if those things never happened. Well, we can't. The things from our pasts happened and had an impact on who we are. But they don't have to define us or control us, and they don't have to be a stain that will never go away.

Salvation makes us new. Jesus's perfect sacrifice in our place erased the stain of sin. The things we have done and have been done to us are gone.

> Therefore, if anyone is in Christ, he is a new creation. The old has passed away; behold, the new has come. (2 Corinthians 5:17 ESV)

The Bible is full of these reassurances:

> The steadfast love of the Lord never ceases; His mercies never come to an end; they are new every morning; great is Your faithfulness. (Lamentations 3:22–24 ESV)

> But God, being rich in mercy, because of the great love with which he loved us, even when we were dead in our trespasses, made us alive together with Christ—by grace you have been saved. (Ephesians 2:4–5 ESV)

> He put a new song in my mouth, a song of praise to our God. Many will see and fear and trust in the Lord. (Psalm 40:3 ESV)

> He who sat on the throne said, "Behold, I am making all things new. Also he said, "Write this down, for these words are trustworthy and true." (Revelation 21:5 ESV)

I hope you have experienced new life in Christ. I am so thankful for the lessons I've learned from my past, but I am even more thankful that Jesus erased the sin and hurt of my past and made everything new. Like Mr. Clean's Magic Eraser on my bathroom floor, Jesus is the only answer for the stain of sin. I hope, if you haven't met him, you will. Only he can make you new and keep you spotlessly clean.

Disclaimer: Do *not* e-mail me with the secret to the Magic Eraser. I want to keep it magical.

Project Jetway

Last week's trip to California took me through four different airports. What a great opportunity for people watching, one of my favorite activities. I don't understand some travelers. Kudos to those who wear comfortable clothing, easy on/off shoes, and are ready for the security checkpoint.

The problem is, there is a fairly large number of travelers who make me wonder what they were thinking. Did they forget they were going to the airport when they got dressed that morning? Did they not think about getting through security and sitting on a plane? I just don't get it.

I saw a deluge of women wearing very short skirts. Why? You are going to spend the majority of your time sitting down. I wear skirts, so I know that when you sit, the skirt rides up. And it seems the shorter and tighter, the more it rises. Then when you stand up after a long flight, it's not exactly a piece of cake to pull that skirt back into its original position, especially if you can't stand up straight until you are in the aisle. I don't get it.

Besides the impracticality, some were just wrong, a fashion faux pas at best. One of those extrashort, supertight skirts was a yellow plaid with matching cap. Maybe she was on her way to work at one of those Irish pubs…by plane.

Lace-up, knee-high boots. You have to take them off to go through security. To make matters worse, you wear them with very tight pants, making it much more difficult to bend over far enough to get the boots off. I hate to see you struggle. At my age, I'd probably break a hip trying to get them off. Maybe I could just ride through the x-ray machine with them on. I don't get it.

Metal hair clips, dozens of them—yes, it's very colorful and a nice style for you, but really, you didn't think about security, did you? Yes, you have to take them out. Yes, all of them. Yes, that holds up the line. Again, where did you think you were going? And the jewelry too. Not to be outdone by the amount of metal in your hair, the bling hanging on every part of your body may make our plane overweight, delaying our flight. I don't get it.

Heavy coats. I often fly in the winter from Philly. I leave my winter coat in the car and run into the terminal before being flash frozen. I can understand taking your winter coat with you if you are flying to another wintery climate. (Don't do that. Go somewhere warm.) But last week, I flew through Phoenix, Arizona, in September. It was the people leaving Phoenix wearing the parkas, wearing them, not carrying them. I don't get it. Are they already freezing? If they are freezing in Phoenix, their only destination should be Death Valley.

Then there was the sixty-something guy dressed in shorts, some sort of character crew socks, loafers, a brightly colored golf shirt, and a fake-straw bowler-style hat. This guy had done a lot right, even though he has clearly never watched a single episode of *What Not to Wear*. He looked comfortable. He wore easy-on, easy-off shoes. He wasn't carrying anything that looked suspicious, eliminating a holdup in security.

The problem here is that his kids aren't going to pick him up at his destination. They will see him at the curb, waving and jumping, and they will keep moving, circling around and around. They will ignore him until all other travelers are gone and no one can see that this man is with them. Guaranteed his checked bag has some identifying mark, like his initials printed in red on an eight-by-eleven laminated sheet of paper, attached with bright orange camo duct tape. Trust me. Parents visiting your children, dress not to embarrass.

There were many more that made me laugh, question, shake my head, and wonder aloud. Sometimes I am in such awe, words fall out of my mouth without me realizing until they hit the air. Oops. I used to get mad at these people who would hold up the security line with their coats and laced boots and hair clips. But not anymore. I paid for TSA PreCheck—no removing jackets, shoes, hair clips, or even laptops. Just get in the short line and go. Best travel purchase I have ever made! Come on over, you travel-fashion nightmares. For $85, you can wear whatever you want for the next five years and not hold up anyone else.

> Get ready; be prepared, you and all the hordes gathered about you, and take command of them.
> (Ezekiel 38:7 NIV taken out of context)

Quilting Prayers

Quilts and babies, babies and quilts! My sewing room was littered with fabric strips, triangles, squares, half-square triangles, and various scraps in a rainbow of colors and patterns. All these little pieces of fabric would become six different baby quilts. There were jungle prints, Winnie-the-Pooh prints, paw prints, butterfly prints, even Star Wars prints. I hoped for some magical mice to appear and help get the jobs done, but they were a no-show.

I usually have a quilt project in the works at all times, but between June 1 and September 15, I needed to get six baby quilts made. At times, it seemed I was quilting in my sleep. The unevenness of the stitches proved it! Piecing the tops came together pretty quickly and easily, which for me is saying a lot. Years ago, while looking at a picture of a quilt I was considering making, I commented that it would be hard. My young son responded, "Quilting isn't hard. You just sew the fabric together, rip it apart, and then sew it together again." Clearly, he has watched me piece many a quilt.

Once the top is finished, it's time to get to the business of quilting. I hand quilt all of my quilts, no matter how big. My quilting friends have a saying, "it all comes out in the quilting." If points or seams didn't match up perfectly or there were other piecing mistakes, they can be fixed or at least hidden in the quilting. No quilt is without flaws, but that's what makes it unique, kind of my signature.

Taking a deep breath, I remind myself that there will be pain, but it will turn out beautiful. You see, I have a tendency to stab myself regularly while quilting. Callouses grow on the tips of my fingers. The good thing is, as the callouses thicken, stabbing my fingers becomes less painful.

Making so many quilts, I started a new tradition. As I sit and quilt in each stitch, I pray for the baby and the parents. The frequent stabbings tell me that there will be painful times for the families receiving this quilt, and I pray for them. Quilting a baby-sized quilt usually takes about two weeks, depending on the detail involved. That's two weeks of praying for a family and new baby—what a privilege and a blessing.

A picture hangs in my sewing room that reads, "Families are like quilts…lives pieced together, stitched with smiles and tears, colored with memories, and bound by love." Many of the quilts in my house came from my husband's great-grandmothers. His mom would point out the fabrics that she remembered, one of her dresses, her father's shirt, her mother's apron, etc. It makes them even more special.

I am the only one in my generation who quilts, but that young, smart aleck son of mine is now all grown up and made a beautiful quilt for his wife that adorns their bed. My three-year-old granddaughter loves to help me tear fabric into strips, and she helped mark the quilting pattern on the last baby quilt. Maybe the tradition will continue for a few more generations.

More importantly than the quilts that are passed from generation to generation, I pray that the love of our heavenly Father will also be passed down.

Nothing warms a grandmom's heart like hearing her grandchild sing praise to God (snuggled under the warmth of a pretty quilt!).

> We always thank God, the Father of our Lord
> Jesus Christ, when we pray for you. (Colossians
> 1:3)

Poop Lasagna

Yup, we're talking poop. I live with a puppy, a newborn, and two toddlers still in diapers. "Who pooped?" is a question heard several times a day. Hang with me, it will be all right.

We have lived in our new house for almost four weeks. During that time, we have had four snowstorms. One of the things we haven't exactly figured out is where the dogs ought to poop. Because of all the snow, the poop area became right outside the front door. Our puppy has to "empty" while on a leash. That means that somebody, usually me, has to be holding the other end of the leash. So I stand at the edge of the front walk while the puppy finds a good spot to empty, and that way, I don't have to walk in the snow.

Because snow comes with a lot of coldness, I don't stay outside long or trek into the snow to pick up the poop right away. Before I knew it, there was a lot of poops. And then it would snow again, covering the dark-contrasting piles. It has become something of a poop lasagna with alternating layers of poop and snow.

Over the last few days, some melting occurred, and lots of poop was exposed. How gross. I decided to scoop up as much as possible since it was trash day and another storm was on the way.

Unfortunately, most of the poop was so frozen to the snow/ice underneath; I couldn't get much of it up. I pried. I pulled. I tried to dig underneath. It wasn't budging. I gave up, looking at the piles of frozen poop in disgust. But the next day, it would all be hidden again under a fresh layer of snow. How convenient. But at some point, it will all come to the surface and have to be reckoned with.

I looked over the poop lasagna in my front yard and thought what a great picture of sin. Sometimes I get rid of it as soon as it is exposed. But too often I just let it get frozen in place and promise to deal with it later, especially the "lesser" sins, like worry, ingratitude, or selfishness.

But the longer I let it go, the more solidly embedded in my heart it becomes. The cleanup can be a long, difficult process. Sometimes it takes some serious prying and chipping away. But God's Word says that he will make my sin as white as snow. It's not that a pristine layer of snow hides it, like the poop lasagna. Jesus actually removes it as if it had never been there. I can start fresh, clean, like new-fallen snow.

> Come now, let us reason together, says the LORD:
> though your sins are like scarlet, they shall be as
> white as snow; though they are red like crimson,
> they shall become like wool. (Isaiah 1:18 ESV)

Three-year-old Emma asked me to put Christmas music on because she wanted to dance. I did and she started running in circles.

Me: Why are you running in circles? I thought you were going to dance.

Emma: Running is dancing when there is music.

Me: Oh, I'm glad you explained that.

* * * * *

A barefooted Emma sat in the Walmart shopping cart at the checkout. An elderly gentleman in line next to us asked her, "Did you lose your shoes?"

"No, I peed in them." He was aghast. What can I say? Ask an almost-three-year-old a question, expect an honest answer.

* * * * *

Three-year-old Everlee came in the kitchen and asked: Where is Daddy?

Mom-mom: He's upstairs giving your little brother a bath.

She starts to go up the stairs.

Pop-pop: Where are you going?

Everlee: I'm going upstairs to get Daddy.

Pop-pop: What do you need Daddy for?

Everlee: No, Daddy needs ME.

* * * * *

Pulling into the bank drive-thru:

Teller: Good morning. How can I help you today?

Two-year-old Emma from the backseat: French fries!

About the Illustrator

Karissa Murmylo has been practicing visual arts since her early childhood and is now a self-made artist. In 2021, Karissa received an honorable mention from the Echo Lake Collaborative for the arts. Her primary art mediums are watercolor, charcoal, pencil, and woodburning. Karissa designs holiday cards and sells a variety of art locally.

About the Author

Lisa Radcliff is an author, speaker, and women's ministry leader in Southeastern Pennsylvania. Her book, *Hidden with Christ: Breaking Free from the Grip of Your Past*, reveals her personal story of childhood sexual abuse and the freedom she found in Christ. Lisa has been a homeschool mom, had a long career with The Seeing Eye Inc., in the puppy development department, and now writes and speaks full-time.

So many people who read her story asked how she can be so full of joy. That was the impetus for writing *A Time to Laugh*. Turning fifty brought about all the typical issues associated with aging but put in the perspective of 2 Corinthians 4:17 ESV: "For this light momentary affliction is preparing for us an eternal weight of glory beyond all comparison." Lisa found laughter even in difficult circumstances.

Lisa also enjoys quilting, shopping, traveling, cheering on Philly sports teams, and spending time with family and friends. She and husband, Doug, have three married sons and nine grandchildren who bring more joy than seems possible in this life. The quinquagenarians in the book are real friends who provide so much laughter and blog fodder. Lisa is very grateful to God for the amazing family and friends he has given to walk with her along life's journey. You can connect with Lisa at her website, www.lisajradcliff.com.

www.ingramcontent.com/pod-product-compliance
Lightning Source LLC
Chambersburg PA
CBHW031313160726
47993CB00001B/406